Hans-Jürgen Schönig
Ewald Geschwinde

Mono

KICK START

S0-BZE-437

SAMS

800 East 96th Street, Indianapolis, Indiana 46240 USA

Mono Kick Start

International Standard Book Number: 0672325799

Library of Congress Catalog Card Number: 2003103986

Printed in the United States of America

First Printing: September 2003

06   05   04   03   4   3   2   1

Trademarks

Warning and Disclaimer

Bulk Sales

Sams Publishing offers excellent discounts on this book when ordered in quantity for bulk purchases or special sales. For more information, please contact

U.S. Corporate and Government Sales
1-800-382-3419
corpsales@pearsontechgroup.com

For sales outside of the U.S., please contact

International Sales
+1-317-428-3341
international@pearsontechgroup.com

Acquisitions Editor
Shelley Johnston

Development Editor
Damon Jordan

Managing Editor
Charlotte Clapp

Project Editor
Dan Knott

Copy Editor
Mike Henry

Indexer
Ken Johnson

Proofreader
Eileen Dennie

Technical Editor
Dietmar Maurer
Dick Porter

Team Coordinator
Vanessa Evans

Designer
Gary Adair

Page Layout
Bronkella Publishing

Contents at a Glance

Table of Contents

Get in Touch with the Authors

If you want to get in touch with us, feel free to send us an email. Tell us what you like and what you don't like about this book. Don't hesitate to send mail to hs@cybertec.at or check out www.cybertec.at. We'll try to answer all of your questions.

Remember, your comments will help us to write better books.

Dedication

This book is dedicated to Ewald Geschwinde's son, Dominik Geschwinde, who was born in 2002.

Acknowledgments

After months of hard work, this book has finally come to life. It is time to say thank you to all the people who accompanied us while working on the manuscript. We want to say thank you to Boris Karnikowski and Dietmar Maurer, who did most of the work for the original Austrian version of this book.

We'd also like to say thank you to everybody who worked on the English version of this book, particularly Shelley Johnston, who did a wonderful job and helped us to achieve our goal of publishing one of the first Mono books on the market.

Nearly a year after we started writing the manuscript for the Austrian version of this book, we can finally provide an English introduction to Mono. We hope that this book will help many people take advantage of working with Mono.

We Want to Hear from You!

As the reader of this book, *you* are our most important critic and commentator. We value your opinion and want to know what we're doing right, what we could do better, what areas you'd like to see us publish in, and any other words of wisdom you're willing to pass our way.

You can email or write me directly to let me know what you did or didn't like about this book—as well as what we can do to make our books stronger.

Please note that I cannot help you with technical problems related to the topic of this book, and that due to the high volume of mail I receive, I might not be able to reply to every message.

When you write, please be sure to include this book's title and author as well as your name and phone or email address. I will carefully review your comments and share them with the author and editors who worked on the book.

Email: opensource@samspublishing.com

Mail: Mark Taber
         Associate Publisher
         Sams Publishing
         800 East 96th Street
         Indianapolis, IN 46240 USA

Reader Services

For more information about this book or others from Sams Publishing, visit our Web site at www.samspublishing.com. Type the ISBN (excluding hyphens) or the title of the book in the Search box to find the book you're looking for.

Introduction

With the introduction of .NET and C#, Microsoft has finally declared war on Sun Microsystems. C# is an interesting alternative to Java and provides a rich set of features that people need to implement modern applications.

The target of the Mono project is to provide a free implementation of Microsoft's .NET Framework. In addition to development tools such as a free C# compiler, Mono offers a set of classes to help the programmer quickly port .NET applications to Mono.

This book is dedicated to all developers who want to get in touch with Mono. We present the system in a simple and easy-to-understand way. We start our tour with the installation of Mono on Windows and Unix platforms. After that, we deal with C# and the differences between Mono and .NET.

Later chapters explain such advanced technologies as network programming and threads. With the help of examples, you'll see where you need to be careful and which features can be used safely.

We hope that this book helps you understand the benefits of the technology. If you have questions, feel free to send an email to office@cybertec.at or check out www.cybertec.at.

In the Beginning, There Was Nothing

In the beginning, there was nothing. That's how people can see the situation as it was some time ago, but in the meantime, the Mono project has gained ground and many new features have been added to the framework.

As we have already mentioned, the target of the Mono project is to provide a free implementation of Microsoft's .NET Framework. One of the highest priorities is to obtain compatibility with .NET. After you've dealt with Mono, .NET, and C#, you'll see that the Mono development community sticks very closely to Microsoft's specifications. That's not always simple and it's a huge challenge for everybody working on the product.

Miguel de Icaza is the father of many open source projects. The most famous project of these is the Gnome project. Gnome is a free and widely used desktop environment based on X.

Because Miguel needed an efficient platform for developing software, he started working on the C# compiler that became the basis of the Mono framework.

Ximian is a company that dedicates a great deal of its work to the Mono project. Ximian provides a number of programmers working actively on the core components of Mono. Meanwhile, there is also a huge community supporting Ximian and Miguel de Icaza. Because C# is an attractive platform for writing new software, the Mono project has gained many new developers. The target of the development is clear, so there isn't much discussion about the final concepts. This leads to a fast evolution of Mono's core components.

Mono and .NET Technologies

After that short introduction to the Mono framework, it's time to have a closer look at the technical details.

Mono consists of various components:

- C# compiler: The C# compiler is the core component of Mono. The compiler is *self-hosting*, which means that it's possible to compile the C# compiler under itself. This is a major milestone in the evolution and development of Mono because the code has become far more independent.

- Common language runtime just-in-time compiler: A just-in-time (JIT) compiler translates intermediate code to optimized platform-dependent code. In contrast to an interpreter, a JIT compiler creates a binary image of the program. Future versions of Mono will provide an AOT compiler as well.

- Classes and modules: The Mono framework provides a rich set of classes. Microsoft has proposed the structure of these classes and the Mono project has tried to fulfill this proposal. Currently, not all classes have been implemented completely but a major part can already be used in production environments. It's important to mention that the classes proposed by Microsoft are part of the ECMA standard.

Common Language Runtime

The core of Mono and .NET is the common language runtime. With the help of the common language runtime, it's possible to develop programs in different programming languages and execute them with just one tool. In case of Mono, that means every tool that generates common language runtime code can be executed using tools provided by Mono.

Microsoft has the same strategy: The idea is that every customer can choose the programming language he likes best. Because every compiler produces common language runtime code, components can be connected with each other no matter which language is used to implement a module. Instead of implementing an assembler backend for every language, Microsoft unified its strategies. This strategy has many advantages: Porting to a new platforms means only the runtime has to be ported. The common language runtime code is always the same, so applications need not be ported anymore. Mono is an open source implementation of .NET, so its strategy is the same.

Managed Code

An important concept that's strongly related to the common language runtime is managed code. *Managed* code means that code is executed under the control of the runtime environment. This restricts the way an application works, but leads to higher security because an application cannot execute dangerous operations anymore.

The list of restrictions an application has to face does not affect application programmers too much because the compiler manages things to a large extent. However, you still have to take care of some things. We'll look at the most interesting subjects later on.

Platform Independent

With the help of .NET, it's possible to implement a module in any language supporting the common language runtime. In case of Mono, this isn't possible yet because only a C# compiler is currently available. In the near future, the community will provide further compilers. Compilers are no longer independent tools—they can be seen as a syntax front end to a large pool of functions. All languages have the chance to access a common set of classes. This leads to a situation in which every programming language has the same power and the same features. It's no longer necessary to implement the same piece of software in every language. In future versions of Mono, users will see the real benefits of this standardization.

To guarantee that every programming language can access every component and to make sure that a module is platform independent, Microsoft has introduced an additional layer called MSIL (*Microsoft Intermediate Language*; according to ECMA specs, it's CIL or *Common Intermediate Language*). CIL code is similar to assembly code. Every compiler is supposed to generate MSIL code. The JIT compiler takes the MSIL code and makes highly optimized, platform-dependent code out of it so that it can be executed efficiently. MSIL code is extremely powerful, and every compiler uses a subset of the features provided by the MSIL.

The Mono framework is built on MSIL as well. Let's have a look at an example that shows what MSIL code looks like:

```
using System;

class   Demo
{
        public static void Main()
        {
                Console.WriteLine("Hello Developer");
        }
}
```

The program displays text on the screen. After compiling the software, we can see the CIL code that's created by using a program named monodis. Calling monodis displays the CIL code of an application on screen:

```
.assembly extern mscorlib
{
  .ver 1:0:3300:0
}
.assembly 'a'
{
  .hash algorithm 0x00008004
  .ver  0:0:0:0
}
  .class private auto ansi beforefieldinit Demo
        extends [mscorlib]System.Object
  {

    // method line 1
    .method public hidebysig  specialname  rtspecialname
          instance default void .ctor()  cil managed
    {
        // Method begins at RVA 0x20ec
        // Code size 7 (0x7)
        .maxstack 8
        IL_0000: ldarg.0
```

```
    IL_0001: call instance void valuetype [corlib]System.Object::.ctor()
    IL_0006: ret
} // end of method instance default void .ctor()


// method line 2
.method public static
        default void Main()  cil managed
{
    // Method begins at RVA 0x20f4
    .entrypoint
    // Code size 11 (0xb)
    .maxstack 8
    IL_0000: ldstr "Hello Developer"
    IL_0005: call void class [corlib]System.Console::WriteLine(string)
    IL_000a: ret
} // end of method default void Main()


} // end of type Demo
```

As we've already seen, the code is very similar to assembly code. In contrast to assembly code, MSIL code is stack based. Nowadays, most assembly language is register based.

Data Types

One tremendous advantage of the Mono framework is the way in which data types are managed. There's a huge set of data types that can be used by all programming languages supported by the framework. If a programmer needs more data types, it's no problem to add an additional data type. These data types can be used just like the predefined data types. This is an enormous advantage because it's possible to implement self-consistent applications.

Assemblies

Mono offers an important concept known as an *assembly*. Assemblies solve many problems Unix and Windows users have to face quite often. Many problems on Unix and Windows are similar, so Mono and the .NET Framework try to solve this problem once and forever.

Many of you know of problems that occur because of inconsistent classes. When somebody writes an application, it might happen that a module will be overwritten. This leads to ugly problems that cannot be fixed easily. Application developers have to face the fact that such problems cannot be fixed because they have no idea which module was substituted for a wrong piece of software. When installing software, a module need not be registered in the system.

The .NET Framework makes sure that no version of a module can be overwritten anymore: Every time an application is launched, it can be absolutely sure that all modules are in place. In the case of Unix, this concept isn't that important because many libraries are available in many versions anyway. Just as .NET does, Mono supports assemblies.

Compatibility

The Mono developers try to make sure that Mono is fully .NET compliant. Not only the compiler is supposed to be .NET compliant; the class libraries should be a counterpart as well. Currently, many classes have already been fully implemented. However, there are still major challenges to be faced. In particular, Windows-specific features will require a lot of work in the future.

Not surprisingly, the C# compiler is the core component of the Mono framework. For some time now, the C# compiler has been self-hosting. This is a major breakthrough in the development of Mono. In recent versions, the code generated by Mono is not very optimized. In future versions, this will most certainly change. A lot of effort will be put into the software to guarantee high performance. Still, the output of Mono's C# compiler can be compared with the output of Microsoft's compiler.

Still, for many applications, Mono can already be used as a serious alternative to .NET. Especially when applications should work on Windows and Unix platforms, Mono is definitely a good choice. In many cases, Mono is even a better choice than Java.

In Brief

- The target of the Mono project is to provide a .NET-compliant programming environment.

- Mono is currently developed by a company called Ximian and many volunteers.

- With the help of Mono, it's possible to implement platform-independent code.

- Mono's C# compiler produces common language runtime code.

- A just-in-time (JIT) compiler translates intermediate code to highly optimized native machine code.

- Mono is fully .NET compliant.

Installation

In the past few months, the installation process of Mono has changed significantly. Back in the early days, it was a big burden to install all the components people normally need to work with Mono. Installing the compiler and the classes that are distributed with Mono used to be particularly complicated. But since then, setting up the system has become very easy.

Currently, Mono can be used on Linux as well as Windows systems on *x*86 CPUs.

Unix

As we have already mentioned, Mono is a free implementation of the .NET Framework. Although Mono is available for Windows platforms, Unix is the more widespread operating system for Mono. In this section, we discuss how Mono can be installed on Linux systems.

Installing Binaries

The fastest way to install Mono on Linux is to use RPM packages. RPM is a system provided by Red Hat, which is widely used on Linux. Today, many Linux distributions rely on RPM packages. Even on modern RS/6000 machines, RPM can be used (in combination with AIX and Linux).

RPM packages for Mono can be downloaded from www. go-mono.org. To install the binaries, you can use

```
[root@localhost monorpm]# ls
libgc-6.1-1.i386.rpm  libgc-devel-6.1-1.i386.rpm
mono-XXX.i386.rpm mono-devel-XXX.i386.rpm
```

Let's install the packages:

```
[root@localhost monorpm]# rpm -Uvh *rpm
Preparing...              ############################### [100%]
   1:libgc                ############################### [ 25%]
   2:libgc-devel          ############################### [ 50%]
   3:mono                 ############################### [ 75%]
   4:mono-devel           ############################### [100%]
```

As you can see, installing packages is really easy. Let's have a look at the options we have just used:

- -U (Update): Updates or installs the desired packages. In contrast to the -i flag, -U updates or installs packages. -i is for installing only.

- -v (Verbose): Makes RPM display some information.

- -h (Hash): Displays hashes to see the progress of the installation.

If no error has occurred, Mono has been installed successfully. To see whether Mono has already been installed, you can use the following command:

```
[root@localhost monorpm]# rpm -qva ¦ grep mono
mono-0.21
mono-devel-0.21
```

The preceding command retrieves all packages installed on the system and looks for the string mono.

Source RPMs

If you want to compile Mono yourself, you can install RPM source packages. After download-ing the source RPMs, they can be installed just as we've done before:

```
[root@localhost tmp]# ls *rpm
libgc-6.1-1.src.rpm  mono-0.21.src.rpm
[root@localhost tmp]# rpm -Uvh *rpm
   1:libgc                ############################### [100%]
   2:mono                 ############################### [100%]
[root@localhost tmp]#
```

When installing source RPMs, the system installs the *spec* files, which are necessary for telling the compiler what to do. Let's look and see where the spec files are installed:

```
[root@localhost SPECS]# pwd
/usr/src/redhat/SPECS
```

```
[root@localhost SPECS]# ls
lame.spec  libgc.spec  mono.spec
```

Compiling the source code is not difficult:

```
[root@localhost SPECS]# rpm -ba *
error: failed build dependencies:
        nasm is needed by lame-3.92-1
```

RPM checks whether all required packages have been installed on the system. If this is not the case, an error occurs. In our example (RedHat 8.0), a package called nasm is missing. If your system raises this error as well, you can download the missing package from http://sourceforge.net:

```
[root@localhost SPECS]# rpm -Uvh /tmp/nasm-0.98.35-1.i386.rpm
Preparing...               ################################# [100%]
   1:nasm                   ################################# [100%]
```

To compile the software just use rpm -bi. If this works for you, Mono has been installed properly.

CVS and Friends

To install the most recent version of Mono, you can use a CVS snapshot. If you aren't a developer, you can download the code anonymously. Three servers can be used: anoncvs-spain-1.go-mono.com, anoncvs-spain-2.go-mono.com, and anoncvs-us-1.go-mono.com.

You'll need three commands to connect to a CVS server:

```
export CVSROOT=:pserver:anonymous@anoncvs.go-mono.com:/mono
cvs login
cvs -z3 co mcs mono gtk-sharp
```

You won't need a password. After a few minutes, the sources will be on your machine:

```
[root@localhost src]# ls
gtk-sharp  mcs  mono
```

If you've already downloaded source code before, it can be updated easily:

```
export CVSROOT=:pserver:anonymous@anoncvs.go-mono.com:/mono
cvs -z3 update -dP mcs mono gtk-sharp
```

Now we can compile the code using autogen/configure, make, and make install. To find more information about this topic, you can check out http://www.go-mono.org/download.html.

An error might occur during the compilation process. Keep in mind that you're compiling a work in progress and not a stable release.

Windows

Mono is an alternative to .NET. Therefore, it can be used on Windows platforms as well. Installing Mono on Windows is easy, so in most cases the user does not face severe troubles.

The Mono development team provides an easy-to-use Windows installer, shown in Figures 2.1, 2.2, and 2.3.

After downloading the installer, everything works nearly automatically. All you have to do is to follow the instructions on screen. The way the installer works changes from time to time and the user interface is continually improving.

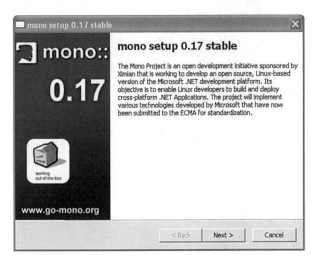

FIGURE 2.1   Installing Mono. Just click the Next button.

During the installation process, a path has to be defined.

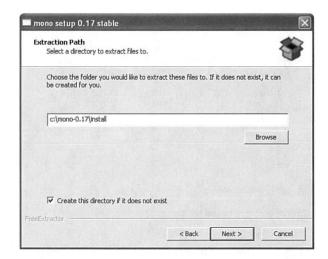

FIGURE 2.2   Installing again. Define the path where you want to install Mono.

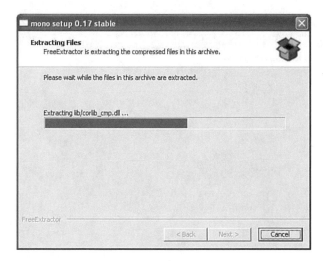

FIGURE 2.3   Mono installs its files.

In general, everything works out fine. After the installation process, you can use Mono safely.

Other Systems

Currently, Mono can be used on Linux, FreeBSD, and Windows (XP, 2000, NT). There are serious attempts to port the framework to other platforms. Because there isn't much Linux-specific stuff in Mono's source code, the development community does not expect many problems when porting Mono to other platforms.

In Brief

- Mono can be used on Linux, FreeBSD, and Windows NT.
- On Windows, you can use a simple menu-driven installer to install Mono on your machine.
- On RPM-based systems, you can use RPM packages to install Mono.
- If you don't want to install the binary version of Mono, you can compile the sources.
- To get the most recent developer version of Mono, you can download a CVS snapshot.
- Additional modules, such as GTK# and Qt#, must be downloaded separately because they are not distributed with the code distribution.

Introducing C#

3

In this chapter, we deal with the core component of Mono. The C# compiler is one of the most powerful tools available. It isn't just a tool for developing applications—it's more. Mono itself is based on C#. This shows the importance of C# when talking about Mono and .NET.

Let's examine C# and see how simple applications can be easily implemented.

Simple Applications

Many books start with an application called Hello World. Let's stick to this good old tradition and let's see how Hello World can be implemented using C#:

```csharp
using System;

class    Hello
{
        public static void Main()
        {
                Console.WriteLine("Hello World\n");
        }
}
```

At the beginning of the program, we include the System namespace. We'll need this module to display text on screen. After that we define a class called Hello. This class contains a function called Main. The C programmers among you will know that the main function is the one that's called at the beginning of a program. In our case, the program does nothing other than display a simple piece of text. This example uses the Console object and the WriteLine method.

After implementing the application, we have to compile it with the help of the C# compiler. The next listing shows how this works:

```
[hs@localhost csharp]$ mcs hello.cs
Compilation succeeded
```

mcs is called to compile hello.cs. The output of this process is an EXE file. To execute the program, you can use mono:

```
[hs@localhost csharp]$ mono hello.exe
Hello World
```

As you can see, you just have to call mono. mono is the just-in-time (JIT) compiler that translates our binary to native code. Alternatively, we could use mint to start the program:

```
[hs@localhost csharp]$ mint hello.exe
Hello World
```

In contrast to mono, mint is an interpreter that evaluates ECMA-CLI code at runtime. Having both programs is a big advantage because mint can be used to debug the C# compiler.

After that first example, it's time to have a look at a slightly modified version of the software:

```
using System;

class    Hello
{
        public static void Main()
        {
                Console.Write("Hello World");
        }
}
```

In this case, we use Write instead of WriteLine. Also, we remove the linefeed.

```
[hs@localhost csharp]$ mcs hello2.cs
Compilation succeeded
[hs@localhost csharp]$ mono hello2.exe
Hello World[hs@localhost csharp]$
```

The output is now two lines longer. If you're planning to write applications that are platform independent, we recommend using WriteLine instead of Write to display linefeeds because the Unix way of starting a new line is platform specific. Beginning a new line is different on every system, so it's better to let C# do the job for you in order to achieve a high abstraction.

An important point to be made about C# is that it's case sensitive, which means that it makes a significant difference whether or not a word is spelled in capital letters. Let's have a look at the next example:

```
using System;

class   Hello
{
        public static void main()
        {
                console.writeline("Hello World");
        }
}
```

The compiler will report an error because a part of the program is spelled the wrong way:

```
[hs@localhost csharp]$ mcs hello3.cs
hello3.cs(7) error CS0103: The name 'console.writeline' could not be
found in 'Hello'
Compilation failed: 1 error(s), 0 warnings
```

As you can see in the listing, the compiler displays a warning and an error. Many of you will have seen this performance when working with other programming languages.

Data Types

An important part in the life of a C# programmer is the management of data types. Just as in C and C++, every variable has a fixed data type. Every data type provides a rich set of operators that can be used to perform a very special operation. Objects can be seen as data types as well, but we'll take a closer look at that later in this book.

Predefined Data Types

C# supports a list of predefined data types. In this section, we examine the most important types. Table 3.1 contains an overview.

TABLE 3.1

Predefined Data Types

C#	MONO	SIGNED	MEMORY	RANGE
sbyte	System.Sbyte	Yes	1 byte	−128 to 127
short	System.Int16	Yes	2 bytes	−32768 to 32767
int	System.Int32	Yes	4 bytes	−2147483648 to 2147483647

TABLE 3.1

Continued

C#	MONO	SIGNED	MEMORY	RANGE
long	System.Int64	Yes	8 bytes	–9223372036854775808 to 9223372036854775807
byte	System.Byte	No	1 byte	0 to 255
ushort	System.Uint16	No	2 bytes	0 to 65535
uint	System.Uint32	No	4 bytes	0 to 4294967295
ulong	System.Uint64	No	8 bytes	0 to 18446744073709551615
float	System.Single	Yes	4 bytes	$-1.5 \times 10\text{-}45$ to $3.4 \times \times 1038$
double	System.Double	Yes	8 bytes	$-5.0 \times 10\text{-}324$ to 1.7×10308
decimal	System.Decimal	Yes	12 bytes	$1.0 \times 10\text{-}28$ to 7.9×1028
char	System.Char		2 bytes	Unicode characters
boolean	System.Boolean		1 byte	True or false

After this brief overview, we'll show you how variables and data types can be used efficiently. The following example shows how a variable can be declared and displayed on screen:

```
using System;

class   Hello
{
        public static void Main()
        {
                int x = 3;
                Console.WriteLine("The value is " +  x );
        }
}
```

Declaring a variable works just like in C and C++. The way data is displayed is reminiscent of Java. We use the plus operator to connect two strings with each other. The output is not surprising:

```
[hs@localhost csharp]$ mono hello4.exe
The value is 3
```

Using the plus operator is truly easy, but it could also be a danger. In most cases, the plus operator is used as a mathematical operator. If it's used differently, the result might be a bit unexpected:

```
using System;
```

```
class    Hello
{
        public static void Main()
        {
                uint x = 3;
                Console.WriteLine("The value is " +  x + 1 );
                Console.WriteLine("The value is " +  (x + 1) );
        }
}
```

We perform two operations that look pretty similar. However, the results differ significantly:

```
[hs@localhost csharp]$ mono hello5.exe
The value is 31
The value is 4
```

The first operation connects two strings. The second example performs an addition. As you can see, the plus operator has more than just one meaning.

One-Dimensional Arrays

It's frequently necessary to store more than just one value in a variable. Fields can be used for this purpose. Arrays are needed to store a set of information. The following example explains how things work:

```
using System;

class    Hello
{
        public static int Main()
        {
                String[] son = { "Hans", "Peter", "Olaf" };
                Console.WriteLine("Son: " + son[0] );

                String[] daughter = new string[3] {
                        "Paula", "Petra", "Clara" };
                Console.WriteLine("Daughter: " + daughter[2] );

                return 1;
        }
}
```

Two arrays are created. Names of men are stored in the first array. To tell Mono that the array called son contains more than just one value, we have to use brackets. To read data in an array, indexes are required. Just as in most other programming languages, the index of an array does not start with 1 but with 0. In the first part of our example, we try to access the array.

The second part of the example shows a slightly different way to create an array. In this case, the size of the array is defined explicitly. Again the elements in the array are accessed using an index. Let's see what comes out when the program is executed:

```
[hs@duron csharp]$ mono array.exe
Son: Hans
Daughter: Clara
```

The values in an array usually aren't static. To modify a value inside an array, the = operator can be called. The next example documents how a value inside an array can be overwritten and how to modify an array:

```
using System;

class   Hello
{
        public static int Main()
        {
                String[] daughter = new string[3] {
                        "Paula", "Petra", "Clara" };
                tochter[2] = "Eva-Maria";
                Console.WriteLine("daughter: " + tochter[2] );

                return 1;
        }
}
```

In this scenario, the third element is replaced with a string that's longer than the original value. The main idea of this example is that you need not worry about memory management anymore because this task is done by Mono. C programmers will know that the operation we've performed is not that simple when using C or C++.

The result is displayed as expected:

```
[hs@duron csharp]$ mono array.exe
daughter: Eva-Maria
```

Multidimensional Arrays

Multidimensional arrays enable the user to implement complex and efficient data structures. Whenever it's necessary to store combinations of different elements, multidimensional arrays are definitely a good idea. C# provides a rich set of sophisticated methods for managing data structures. The following example shows how names can be stored:

```
using System;

class   Hello
{
        public static int Main()
        {
                string[ , ] data = new string[2, 2];

                data[0, 0] = "Paul"; data[1, 0] = "Rudi";
                data[0, 1] = "Ruth"; data[1, 1] = "Evi";

                Console.WriteLine("Value: " + data[1, 1] );

                return 1;
        }
}
```

As you can see in the example, many names are stored in a two-dimensional array. Women can be found in the second axis. The first axis enables us to access the names. The next listing shows what the results look like:

```
[hs@duron csharp]$ mono marray.exe
Value: Evi
```

When working with arrays, it can be interesting to find out how many axes an array contains. In most programming languages, multidimensional data structures are truly painful. However, in C#, those problems have nearly been solved for you because the programming language itself does most of the work. Let's have a look at an additional example:

```
using System;

class   Hello
{
        public static int Main()
        {
```

```
                    string[ , ] a = new string[2, 2];
                    string[ ,,, ] b = new string[2, 2, 2, 2];

                    Console.WriteLine("a: " + a.Rank );
                    Console.WriteLine("b: " + b.Rank );

                    return 1;
            }
    }
```

At the beginning of the program, two arrays are created. The number of axes can be found in a variable called Rank.

Let's see which result we get:

```
[hs@duron csharp]$ mono main.exe
a: 2
b: 4
```

Escaping Characters

In some cases, characters cannot be displayed directly. This can lead to problems. The next line shows what problems might occur:

```
Console.WriteLine("This is a quotation mark: " ");
```

We try to display a quotation mark, which leads to an error because the compiler cannot translate the code. The compiler has no chance to do so because there's no way to find out which quotation mark means what. To tell the C# compiler which character to display on screen, we can use a backslash. In the next example, you can see how the most important symbols can be displayed:

```
using System;

class    Hello
{
        public static void Main()
        {
                Console.WriteLine("Single quote: \'");
                Console.WriteLine("Quotation mark: \"");
                Console.WriteLine("Backslash: \\");
                Console.WriteLine("Alert: \a ");
                Console.WriteLine("Backspace: -\b");
```

```
        Console.WriteLine("Formfeed: \f");
        Console.WriteLine("Newline: \n");
        Console.WriteLine("Carriage Return: \r");
        Console.WriteLine("Tabulator: before\tafter");
        Console.WriteLine("Tab: \v");
        Console.WriteLine("binary  0: \0");
    }
}
```

Backspaces are important—in contrast to other characters, backspaces make it possible to delete other characters. Not all characters lead to real output. In case of binary zeros, nothing is displayed on screen:

```
[hs@localhost csharp]$ mcs hello6.cs; mono hello6.exe
Compilation succeeded
Single quote: '
Quotation mark: "
Backslash: \
Alert:
Backspace: -
Formfeed:

Newline:

Carriage Return:
Tabulator: before        after
Tab:

binary 0:
```

Escaping characters is essential. Particularly when dealing with external data structures, databases, or XML, escaping is important. We'll get back to escaping later in this book.

Symbols for escaping special characters are important when talking about paths. Paths can contain a number of backslashes. Especially on Microsoft Windows systems, this is interesting subject matter that can be the root of evil. Therefore, C# provides a simple mechanism for escaping backslashes in a path. Let's look at an example:

```
using System;

class   Hello
{
        public static void Main()
        {
```

```
        String error = "c:\new_pics";
        Console.WriteLine("Error: " + error + "\n");

        String correct = @"c:\new_pics";
        Console.WriteLine("Correct: " + correct);
    }
}
```

The first string contains a hidden line feed that causes trouble when displaying the text on the screen. In the second example, we use *verbatim* strings—this is a special kind of string that escapes only quotation marks. The advantage of verbatim strings is that the programmer need not worry about symbols other than quotation marks.

Let's see what comes out when the program is started:

```
[hs@localhost mono]$ mono path.exe
Error: c:
ew_pics

Correct: c:\new_pics
```

Flow Control

After this first introduction to C#, we'll examine flow control and control structures. We'll need this information to implement code that is executed only under certain circumstances.

If/Else

Conditional execution is a core component of every programming language. Just like C and C++, C# supports If statements. To see how If statements work, we've implemented a trivial example:

```
using System;

class   Hello
{
        public static void Main()
        {
                int     number = 22;
                if      (number > 20)
                        Console.WriteLine("if branch ...");
                else
                {
```

```
            Console.WriteLine("else branch ...");

        }
    }
}
```

Inside the C# program, we define an integer value. After that the system checks whether the value is higher than 20. If the condition is true, the code inside the If block is executed. Otherwise, the Else branch is called. It's important to mention that the blocks should be marked with parentheses, but this is not a must. Parentheses are normally used to make the code clearer.

When the program is called, one line is displayed:

if branch ...

As we expected, Mono called the If branch.

However, in many real-world scenarios, simple If statements are not enough. It's often useful to combine If statements. When working with Mono and C#, this is no problem:

```
using System;

class    Hello
{
        public static int Main(String[] args)
        {
                Console.WriteLine("Input: " + args[0]);
                if      (args[0] == "100")
                {
                        Console.WriteLine("correct ...");
                        return 0;
                }
                else if (args[0] == "0")
                {
                        Console.WriteLine("not correct ...");
                }
                else
                {
                        Console.WriteLine("error :(");
                }
                return 1;
        }
}
```

This program is supposed to tell us whether a user has entered a correct number. If 0 is passed to the program, we want a special message to be displayed. Our problem can be solved with the help of else if because it can be used to define a condition inside an If statement. The comparison operator demands some extra treatment. As you can see, we use == to compare two values with each other.

Do not use the = operator for checking whether two values are the same. The = operator is used for assigning values it isn't an operator for comparing values. The C and C++ programmers among you already know about this subject matter.

The way data is passed to the program is important as well. The array called args contains all the values that a user passes to the script. Indexing the array starts with zero. Let's see what happens when we call the program with a wrong number:

```
[hs@duron mono]$ mono if.exe 23
Input: 23
error :(
```

In this case, a message is displayed.

Case/Switch **Statements**

Especially when a lot of values are involved, If statements can soon lead to unclear and hard-to-read code. In this case, working with case/switch statements is a better choice. In the next example, we see how the correct translation of a word can be found:

```
using System;

class   Hello
{
        public static int Main()
        {
                String inp;
                String res = "unknown";

                // Reading from the keyboard
                Console.Write("Enter a value: ");
                inp = Console.ReadLine();

                Console.WriteLine("Input: " + inp);

                // Read the translation
                switch(inp)
```

```
            {
                    case "Fernseher":
                            res = "TV";
                            break;
                    case "Honig":
                            res = "honey";
                            break;
                    case "Geschlecht":
                    case "Sex":
                            res = "sex";
                            break;
            }

            Console.WriteLine("Result: " + res);

            return 0;
        }
}
```

First of all, we read a string. To fetch the values from the keyboard, we use the ReadLine method, which is part of the Console object. After reading the value, we call Console.WriteLine and display the value. Now the switch block is entered. All case statements are processed one after the after until the correct value is found.

One thing has to be taken into consideration: A case block is not exited before the system finds a break statement. This is an extremely important concept. If you use switch, case, and break cleverly, it's possible to implement complex decision trees. A good example is the words *Geschlecht* and *Sex*. In German, the words are different, but they have the same English translation. Because we do not use a break in the Geschlecht block, C# jumps directly to the Sex block where the correct word is found. In this block, a break statement is used and so the switch block is exited. Many advanced programmers appreciate this feature.

Let's compile and execute the program:

```
[hs@duron mono]$ mono case.exe
Enter a value: Fernseher
Input: Fernseher
Result: TV
[hs@duron mono]$ mono case.exe
Enter a value: Geschlecht
Input: Geschlecht
Result: sex
```

As you can see, the correct result has been found.

Case/Switch statements also provide default statements. Default values help you to define the default behavior of a block if no proper values are found. Using strings in Switch statements isn't possible in most other language—that's a real benefit of C#.

Goto

Just as in the golden age, Microsoft provides the goto command. Many of you know this feature from ancient versions of the BASIC programming language. C# provides jumps as well. With the help of goto, it's possible to jump to any position inside the program and to continue working there. To find out how this works, we've implemented a trivial example:

```
using System;

class   Hello
{
        public static void Main()
        {
                Console.WriteLine("Paul is married");
                goto nobodyknows;
                Console.WriteLine("Paul plays around with other women");

nobodyknows:
                Console.WriteLine("Paul is in love");
        }
}
```

After processing the first line, the program jumps to nobodyknows. Luckily, those evil things aren't displayed and the output isn't too dangerous for Paul:

```
[hs@duron mono]$ mono ex.exe
Paul is married
Paul is in love
```

Try to avoid jumps when possible; otherwise, your programs will be complex and painful to maintain. It's much better to use functions, but we'll deal with modules later in this book.

Loops

Loops are a fundamental component of every modern programming language. Whenever a set of commands has to be executed more than once, a loop is a good idea and, in many cases, the only choice.

C# provides all fundamental kinds of loops and we take a closer look at them in this section.

while

while loops are a widespread way to perform repeated computation. A while loop is executed as long as a certain condition returns true. The next listing contains a program showing how things work:

```
using System;

class   Loop
{
        public static void Main()
        {
                bool keepdoing = true;
                string input;

                while   (keepdoing == true)
                {
                        Console.Write("Input: ");
                        input = Console.ReadLine();
                        Console.WriteLine("Output: " + input);

                        if      (input.Length < 3)
                                keepdoing = false;
                }
        }
}
```

As an alternative to keepdoing == true, we could have used while (keepdoing). The target of the program is to accept input as long as the user inserts data that's longer than two characters. Therefore, we create two variables. The first one is a flag telling us whether the loop is supposed to keep going. The second variable contains the string provided by the user. The loop is executed as long as keepdoing is true. After the user has entered the new record via his keyboard, we compute the length of the string. If it's too short, we set the flag and the loop terminates. The length of a string can be retrieved using the Length method. This method is part of the class called String—we'll deal with this class extensively later in the book.

The next listing shows what might happen:

```
[hs@duron mono]$ mono while.exe
Input: I am inside
Output: I am inside
```

```
Input: a loop.
Output: a loop.
Input: It is fun to be here.
Output: It is fun to be here.
Input:
Output:
```

After the third input, the program terminates.

When talking about loops, the keyword continue is important. It makes sure that a program can jump directly to the condition of a loop. This feature is nice to have, particularly when implementing blocks that consist of many lines.

do/while

When a loop must be executed at least once, an ordinary while loop just isn't what you're looking for. A do/while loop is easier to implement and is more suitable for this special purpose. The following listing contains a brief example showing the way do/while loops can be used:

```csharp
using System;

class   Loop
{
        public static void Main()
        {
                bool again = true;
                string input;

                do
                {
                        Console.WriteLine("Y: yes");
                        Console.WriteLine("N: no");
                        Console.Write("Input: ");

                        input = Console.ReadLine();
                        Console.WriteLine("Output: " + input);

                        if      (input == "N")
                                again = false;
                } while     (again == true);
        }
}
```

The program displays an interactive menu and checks whether the loop should be processed again. As long as the user doesn't enter N, the program keeps asking for input. It's important to mention that the process is case sensitive, so entering *n* does not terminate the program:

```
[hs@duron mono]$ mono loop.exe
Y: yes
N: no
Input: Y
Output: Y
Y: yes
N: no
Input: Y
Output: Y
Y: yes
N: no
Input: n
Output: n
Y: yes
N: no
Input: N
Output: N
```

do/while loops are normally used to perform far more complex operations. In this book, we try to focus on the most basic and most important facts so that you can get in touch with Mono and C# quickly.

for **Loops**

for loops are an important alternative to while loops. In principle, every operation you can implement with the help of a while loop can be implemented based on a for loop as well. It depends on which loop the programmer likes best and which method is best to achieve a certain target.

In this section, we take a closer look at for loops. Again, let's start with a simple example:

```
using System;

class    MyLoop
{
        public static void Main()
        {
                int i;
                for    (i = 0; i < 6; i++)
                {
```

```
                         Console.WriteLine("current value: " + i);
            }
        }
}
```

Before we get to the loop, we define a variable called i. Inside the loop, we've defined that the first value of i should be 0. Every time the block is executed, i is incremented. Therefore, we use i++. The ++ operator is widespread because it's efficient and many C/C++ programmers are already familiar with this feature. The loop is executed as long as i is less than a specific value. In our case, this value is 6. In this example, we used parentheses around the block we want to execute. This isn't a must, but it makes sure that the program is easier to read and therefore easier to understand. i++ is the same as i = i + 1. The counterpart of i++ is i--. i-- means that i is decremented.

Let's see which result we can expect:

```
[hs@duron mono]$ mono forloop.exe
current value: 0
current value: 1
current value: 2
current value: 3
current value: 4
current value: 5
```

As you can see in the listing, all numbers from 0 to 5 are displayed.

The same target can be achieved with the next piece of code:

```
using System;

class   MyLoop
{
        public static void Main()
        {
                int i;
                for     (i = 0; i < 6; )
                {
                        Console.WriteLine("current value: " + i);
                        i++;
                }
        }
}
```

In this example, we omitted the third argument of the function. Whenever a loop is more complex, this can be essential because the current value of the parameter (in our case, i) might be the result of complex operations. In the example, we've incremented i inside the loop. The result is the same.

foreach

An additional loop provided by C# is the foreach loop. foreach is also commonly used in many programming languages, such as Perl. Whenever it's necessary to process all values in a set one after another, foreach loops are far more comfortable than other kinds of loops.

Let's write a foreach loop and see how all values in an array can be displayed:

```
using System;

class    Loop
{
        public static void Main()
        {
                string[] children = { "Peter", "Paul", "Josef" };
                foreach (string child in children)
                {
                        Console.WriteLine("Child: " + child);
                }
        }
}
```

First, we define an array that contains the names of three children. In the next step, we process every value in the array. Every single value in the field is assigned to child and displayed on screen. This leads to the following result:

```
[hs@duron mono]$ mono children.exe
Child: Peter
Child: Paul
Child: Josef
```

This way, it's truly simple to implement dynamic data structures for storing an undefined amount of data.

Documentation

If source code is the heart of an application, documentation is its soul. Documentation is often neglected and not updated regularly. Especially when the schedule of a project is tight and there isn't much time left, people start to save the time they've lost by cutting the resources for writing documentation.

Mono and C# try to integrate documentation and code in order to minimize the work for a programmer. It's far easier to write documentation inside a program than with the help of an external editor. In addition, documentation that's inside the source is more consistent with the software itself than external texts.

C# relies on XML. Therefore, XML is used to document an application. The next example shows how XML can be used to document a simple application:

```
using System;

class    MyLoop
{
        public static void Main()
        {
                /// <summary>
                ///     This is a free advertisement
                ///     for www.postgresql.at
                /// </summary>
                Console.WriteLine("Check out www.postgresql.at");
                /// <seealso> www.go-mono.org </seealso>
        }
}
```

It's possible to embed XML in any C# application. A rich set of elements are defined, as shown in Table 3.2.

TABLE 3.2

XML Elements

XML ELEMENT	MEANING
<c>	Marks a paragraph as code
<code>	Marks text as code
<doc>	Root element of the XML file
<event>	Describes an event
<example>	Marks an example
<exception>	Defines an exception that a function can provide
<field>	Describes a field
<list>	Defines a list or a table
<method>	Describes a method
<para>	Marks a text as paragraph
<param>	Defines a parameter of a method
<paramref>	Marks a word as parameter
<permission>	Defines user rights

TABLE 3.2
Continued

XML ELEMENT	MEANING
<property>	Defines a property
<remarks>	Adds remarks and important messages
<returns>	Defines the return value of a method
<see>	Defines a link
<seealso>	Points to additional documentation
<summary>	Summary
<type>	Defines a type

In this list, we omitted the corresponding closing tags because they're just as in HTML. For example, the closing tag for <tag> would be </tag>.

Let's see what happens when we execute the program:

```
[hs@duron mono]$ mono ex.exe
Check out www.postgresql.at
```

At the time this text was written, there was no suitable tool for processing the documentation inside a program.

Simple Classes

Up to now, we've dealt with programs consisting of nothing more than simple straightforward functions. Now it's time to get in touch with more complex stuff, so we'll learn to deal with functions and methods. Based on methods, we'll start to implement classes and you'll see how classes can be used to efficiently achieve very specific goals.

Objects and Instances

Some people reading this book might be familiar with object-oriented software development in general and some will already have practical experience. Because we want all readers to benefit from this book, we've dedicated the next section to object-oriented programming and its fundamentals.

Objects are nothing more than data structures, data, and methods for processing the data at once. Objects are templates for a certain piece of data. Every object accepts a set of parameters that define it. The methods of an object can be used only in combination with an object. This leads to an encapsulation of data that is visible only inside the object.

In this section, we take our first look at classes. To get a first impression of objects, it's time to consider an example:

```csharp
using System;

class   Demo
{
        public static void Main()
        {
                Human hugo = new Human();
        }
}

// The class itself
public class    Human
{
        public Human ()
        {
                Console.WriteLine("Born to be alive ...");
        }
}
```

In this example, we use two classes. The class called Demo contains the main function that every C# program starts with. In addition to that, we implement a class named Human, which also consists of just one function. This function is known as a *constructor*. The only target of a constructor is to create new objects. In our case, we call the constructor to generate a variable called hugo. The data type of hugo is Human. To generate additional humans, we could call the constructor more than once.

A constructor must always have the same name as the class it represents. This is an important point because functions that have the wrong name will never be treated as constructors by the compiler. The constructor of the Human object does nothing else than displaying text on the screen. At the end of the program, all variables are deleted automatically.

When working with objects, we must distinguish between objects and instances. Common linguistic usage does not make a big difference between instances and objects, but it's important to understand how things work: Objects are templates that tell us how objects are built and what they look like. A variable generated by a constructor is called an *instance*. To make the difference clearer, we'll explain the main ideas with the help of an example. The class called Human is the construction plan for all humans. Let's see what happens when we start the constructor:

```
[hs@duron mono]$ mono human.exe
Born to be alive ...
```

As you can see, a string is displayed.

Functions and Methods

To access an object, a programmer needs methods. If you want hugo to learn to walk, we have to teach him how this works by implementing a method. In the next example, we teach hugo some nice things:

```csharp
using System;

class   Demo
{
        public static void Main()
        {
                Human hugo = new Human();
                hugo.GrowUp();
                hugo.DrinkBeer();
        }
}

public class    Human
{
        public Human ()
        {
                Console.WriteLine("Hello World ...");
        }

        public void GrowUp ()
        {
                Console.WriteLine("Now I am old enough :) ");
        }

        public void DrinkBeer ()
        {
                Console.WriteLine("I am drinking beer");
        }
}
```

This version of our program supports more than just one constructor. We've implemented two methods that will help us to treat hugo in the way we want him to be treated. In our example, hugo grows up and drinks his first glass of beer. It's important to see how we've implemented these methods. All methods are *public*, which means that they can be called by a method that isn't in our class—in this case, we're talking about the Main function. If we had declared these methods as private, there would be no way for the main program to work with hugo because private methods are not visible inside the main program.

The return value of a method is important as well. In the code we've seen before, all methods return void (undefined). This makes sense because the code does nothing other than displaying text. If we want a method to perform complex operations, we have to choose a data type that can be used to store the desired result.

The output of our program is in no way surprising:

```
[hs@duron mono]$ mono ex.exe
Hello World ...
Now I am old enough :)
I am drinking beer
```

Three lines are displayed.

Variables and Scope

After you've learned how to implement basic classes, we'll take a closer look at variables and scope in general. In addition, we'll deal with constant values.

Constants

If variables must not be changed at runtime, they can be marked as constants. To mark a variable as a constant, the keyword const has to be used.

```
using System;

class    MyConst
{
        public static void Main()
        {
                const double pi = 3.14;
                Console.WriteLine("Pi: " + pi );
        }
}
```

In this case, we cannot change the value of pi; otherwise, the compiler will report an error. This makes sense because many predefined values rely on this feature.

```
[hs@duron mono]$ mono ex.exe
Pi: 3.14
```

Scope—The Basics

Variables are an essential component of every program. However, a variable cannot be seen everywhere inside the program. This is important because otherwise you'd have to invent a new name for every variable in the system. In huge packages, this is nearly impossible.

Therefore, every variable has a certain *scope*, which means that it's available in a clearly defined part of the software. Let's get to some practical stuff and see how the things that we just discussed can be put to work:

```
using System;

class   Demo
{
        public static void Main()
        {
                string name = "Hugo";
                Human hugo = new Human(name);
        }
}

class   Human
{
        public Human(string objname)
        {
                Console.WriteLine("I am " + objname);
                Console.WriteLine("I am " + name);
        }
}
```

In the main function, we define a variable and an instance of Human. The constructor of this object tries to access these variables. Because we haven't declared name inside the class, it cannot be seen, so the compiler reports an error:

```
[hs@duron mono]$ mcs method.cs
ex.cs(17) error CS0103: The name 'name' could not be found in 'Human'
Compilation failed: 1 error(s), 0 warnings
```

As you can see, the desired value is not visible. This is a fundamental concept because every variable and method has a clearly defined scope.

Block and Scope

In some cases, variables cannot be seen in an entire function. It can be useful to restrict the scope even more. This makes sense, particularly in the case of loops or conditions. Even for that purpose, C# provides all you need:

```
using System;

class   Demo
{
```

```
public static void Main()
{
        int i = 3;
        if      (i == 3)
        {
                int j = 25;
        }

        Console.WriteLine("j: " + j );
}
}
```

In this example, we create two variables. The first one can be seen in the entire function. However, j can be seen only inside the If block. If we try to print the content of j outside the If block, the compiler will report an error because it cannot find the correct value.

```
[hs@duron mono]$ mcs ex.cs
ex.cs(13) error CS0103: The name 'j' could not be found in 'Demo'
Compilation failed: 1 error(s), 0 warnings
```

The behavior you just saw is important because it helps the programmer to split the code into logical blocks.

Variables

Until now, we've dealt with objects that consist of nothing more than a constructor and a set of methods. However, in some cases, it's useful to store data directly inside an instance. Let's get back to the class called Human we've seen before. A human being has many attributes, such as name, weight, gender, and so forth. Those values can be assigned to an instance. Let's see how this can be done with the help of a simple C# application:

```
using System;

class    Demo
{
        public static void Main()
        {
                string name = "Hugo";
                double weight = 89.2;

                Human hugo = new Human(name, weight);
                Console.WriteLine("Name: " + hugo.name);
        }
}
```

```
class   Human
{
        public string name;
        double weight;

        public Human(string objname, double objweight)
        {
                this.name = objname;
                this.weight = objweight;
        }
}
```

We define two variables in the definition of the class. One of these values is `public`, but we will deal with this subject later in this chapter. Inside the constructor, we assign the desired values to the class's internal values.

Our instance contains the desired information and it can be easily accessed by using a dot and the name of the class's internal value:

```
[hs@duron mono]$ mono human.exe
Name: Hugo
```

The name is displayed on screen.

In the next example, we try to display the second variable as well. Let's look at the following piece of code:

```
using System;

class   Demo
{
        public static void Main()
        {
                string name = "Hugo";
                double weight = 89.2;

                Human hugo = new Human(name, weight);
                Console.WriteLine("Name: " + hugo.name);
                Console.WriteLine("Name: " + hugo.weight);
        }
}

class   Human
{
```

```
        public string name;
        double weight;

        public Human(string objname, double objweight)
        {
                this.name = objname;
                this.weight = objweight;
        }
}
```

The compiler displays a fatal error:

```
[hs@duron mono]$ mcs human.cs
human.cs(12) error CS0122: 'Human.weight' is inaccessible due to its protection level
Compilation failed: 1 error(s), 0 warnings
```

The reason for the error is simple: Not all variables can be seen from outside. `name` has been declared `public`, so everybody can access it from outside. `weight` can be seen only inside the class itself; therefore, nobody can see it from outside. Protecting variables has many advantages. Especially when your class contains temporary variables that are part of a complex operation, hiding data makes sense.

C# provides an advanced system for defining the scope of variables. The following list is a brief overview of all keywords provided by C#:

- `private`: A variable can be seen only inside the class.

- `protected`: A variable can be seen only inside the class or a derived class.

- `internal`: The variable can be seen inside the same assembly.

- `protected internal`: The variable is visible inside an assembly or a derived class.

- `public`: The variable can be seen outside the class.

The keywords we just discussed enable the programmer to define precisely what can be seen where. It's essential to make use of these keywords to protect your application from disaster.

Functions and Scope

Not only the scope of variables can be limited. Almost everything we've learned about variables can be used for methods as well. With the help of limitations, it's possible to hide functions from the user. Hiding functions can be useful because many classes contain internal functions that must not be exposed to the user for security reasons.

Let's get started with a look at an example:

```
using System;

class    Demo
{
        public static void Main()
        {
                Human hugo = new Human("Hugo");
                hugo.GrowUp();
        }
}

public class    Human
{
        public Human(string name)
        {
                Console.WriteLine(name + " is born ...");
        }

        public void GrowUp()
        {
                this.LearnToRead();
                this.LearnToWrite();
        }

        private void LearnToRead()
        {
                Console.WriteLine("Reading is simple ...");
        }

        private void LearnToWrite()
        {
                Console.WriteLine("Writing is fun ...");
        }
}
```

At the beginning of the program, we create an instance of Human. This time we implement various methods. The method called GrowUp is a public method—all other methods are private and cannot be called from the Main function.

The example will lead to a simple result set:

```
[hs@duron mono]$ mono ex.exe
Hugo is born ...
Reading is simple ...
Writing is fun ...
```

The `GrowUp` method calls both other methods, which need not be seen by the `Main` function because they're called from inside the object.

Methods can be marked with the help of keywords. Let's look at the keywords provided by C#:

- `abstract`: Prototype without implementation.

- `extern`: An external method can be called from modules that are outside the program.

- `intern`: The method can be called only inside the class.

- `New`: Hides a method that has the same name.

- `Override`: Redefines a method that has been marked as virtual in the base class.

- `Private`: The method can be called only inside the class.

- `Protected`: The method can be seen only inside the class or inside a derived class.

- `Static`: Method isn't part of an instance of a certain class.

- `Virtual`: Makes sure that a derived class can be marked as override.

As you've already seen, when talking about methods, it's useful to expose to the user only those functions that are absolutely necessary.

Namespaces—The First Contact

Namespaces are a fundamental concept of C# and .NET. In this section, we take our first look at namespaces and Mono in general.

Fundamentals

Namespaces can be compared with packages. Some of you already know this concept from languages such as Sun's Java. However, there are some fundamental differences that must be discussed: Namespaces are a logical structure—not every namespace has to be in a separate file. The physical organization of files has nothing to do with logical structures. The advantage is that it's no problem to use modules from different vendors without worrying about conflicts between those modules. If namespaces are used properly, conflicts are very unlikely.

To make it short: Namespaces help us to define logical units consisting of classes, variables, and methods.

One of the most important namespaces of Mono and .NET is the System namespace. It contains a set of basic and fundamental classes that you'll need for almost any application based on Mono. If we look at the method called WriteLine, we'll see that it is part of the Console object. As you might expect, this object is part of the System namespace just as many other objects are.

Namespaces can be nested. That means that a namespace can consist of various other namespaces. A good example is the System.Collection namespace. You'll need the System.Collection namespace to manage dynamic data structures.

Using Namespaces

Thinking of namespaces leads to one rudimentary question: When should you define a namespace? Well, the basic idea is relatively simple: Whenever you want to group a set of classes logically, namespaces can make sense. In addition, namespaces make sense when you want to implement an entire software package because it helps you to separate your classes from those of other people. Your product can contain classes that fulfill a certain task—the classes of your business rival will do the same thing. If you use your company's name as the name of your namespace, it's very likely that your software components can coexist with other people's software. If you use namespaces cleverly, you can avoid many nasty problems.

References

Up to now you've seen how basic applications can be implemented easily. In those applications, we accessed variables directly and modified them without worrying about anything else.

However, in many cases, it's necessary to pass values to other procedures. This usually isn't a problem, but in some cases it leads to some new circumstances that you have to deal with:

```
using System;

public class Demo
{
        public static void Main()
        {
                int x = 3;
                int y = 5;

                Swap(x, y);
                Console.WriteLine("x: {0} - y: {1}", x, y);
        }
}
```

```
static void Swap(int a, int b)
{
        int c = a;
        a = b;
        b = c;
        Console.WriteLine("a: {0} - b: {1}", a, b);
}
}
```

We define two variables inside the main program. The target of the method called Swap is to change the content of those values. Both variables are passed to the function. Inside the function, we try to swap the content of the variables. Finally, we display the result. Let's see which result you can expect:

```
[hs@duron csharp]$ mono ref.exe
a: 5 - b: 3
x: 3 - y: 5
```

The values are obviously still in the same order. The reason for that is fairly simple to explain. When Swap is started, both values are allocated on the stack. In other words, the system creates a copy of the two values. We swap the copies and the function is terminated. This does not affect the original data.

To get rid of the problem, we have to use what are known as *references*. The following piece of code shows how the problem can be solved with the help of C:

```
#include <stdio.h>

void swap(int *a, int *b)
{
        int c = *a;
        *a = *b;
        *b = c;
        printf("a: %d - b: %d\n", *a, *b);
}

int main()
{
        int x = 3;
        int y = 5;

        swap(&x, &y);
        printf("x: %d - y: %d\n", x, y);

        return 0;
}
```

The main program passes the address of the variable to the function. The address is the location of a certain piece of data in memory. In that way, the function can access and modify the data directly in memory.

The output of the problem will look like this:

```
[hs@duron csharp]$ gcc ref.c
[hs@duron csharp]$ ./a.out
a: 5 - b: 3
x: 5 - y: 3
```

The system changes the values and displays them on screen. After this small excursion into the world of C, we'll get back to a simple C# application. The following listing shows how the problem we just discussed can be solved by means of C#:

```
using System;

public class Demo
{
        public static void Main()
        {
                int x = 3;
                int y = 5;

                Swap(ref x, ref y);
                Console.WriteLine("x: {0} - y: {1}", x, y);
        }

        static void Swap(ref int a, ref int b)
        {
                int c = a;
                a = b;
                b = c;
                Console.WriteLine("a: {0} - b: {1}", a, b);
        }
}
```

When passing the data to the function, we mark it as a reference. The method accepting the data must know that the variable is a reference, so it has to be mentioned in the head of the function as well. The syntax provided by C# makes it much more pleasant to work with pointers than in C. Many of those among you who have experience with C will know what we're talking about. The source of trouble is minimal and it isn't that easy to induce troubles caused by pointers.

In the next listing, we'll see how variables can be swapped correctly:

```
[hs@duron csharp]$ mono ref.exe
a: 5 - b: 3
x: 5 - y: 3
```

Working with references is easy and does not lead to many troubles. C# and the Mono framework provide pointers as well. We'll talk about pointers when we get to unsafe code and including C code in C# in Chapter 16.

Data Types and Boxing

After our introduction to C#, we continue with an additional topic that's important to most programmers: managing data types.

Value Types and Reference Types

C# provides both value types and reference types. The difference between them is a fundamental concept. In strictly object-oriented languages, every variable is an object. In contrast to variables you might know from procedural languages, objects are far more complex and lead to some overhead. When somebody allocates an integer variable in C/C++, 4 bytes are allocated on the stack. But when an instance of an object is created, far more memory is needed to store all the administrative information.

To raise performance, C# defines a difference between variables storing data (value types) and objects that can be used to store data as well (reference types). References are similar to references in C++. Therefore, references are extremely important because it isn't necessary to pass an entire object to a method. We'll get back to this major difference later in this book.

Boxing

The question now is how the difference between value types and reference types can be used efficiently. One potential scenario is *boxing*. With the help of boxing, it's possible to hide a variable inside an object.

The following example shows how this works:

```
using System;

public class Demo
{
        public static void Main()
        {
```

```
        int a = 42;
        object b = a;
        int c = (int) b;

        Console.WriteLine("c: " + c);
    }
}
```

First, we create an integer variable. After that, the variable is hidden inside an object. To extract the data from the object, we perform a *cast*, which means that we modify the data type of the variable. This can be done by putting the desired data type in brackets. In the following code, you can see the result we can expect:

```
[hs@duron csharp]$ mono box.exe
c: 42
```

With regard to reference types, many programmers get the wrong impression of what they're dealing with. Using a reference type is not the same as using a pointer in C or C++. To make this clear, we've decided to include an example showing that the situation is very different from C:

```
using System;

public class Demo
{
    public static void Main()
    {
        int a = 42;
        object b = a;
        Console.WriteLine("before: " + a);

        Increment(b);
        int c = (int) b;
        Console.WriteLine("after: " + c);
    }

    static void Increment(Object x)
    {
        int y = (int)x;
        y++;
        x = y;
    }
}
```

After creating an integer variable, we put it into an object. It is passed to the `Increment` function. As we just saw, objects are reference types. Inside the function, we take the object and increment its content by one. Finally, the new value is assigned to the object. If we had a pointer (as in C), the result would differ from the one that follows:

```
[hs@duron csharp]$ mono box.exe
before: 42
after: 42
```

Both values are the same. The reason for that is that we do not access the variable in the `Main` function of the program. This is an important concept, and you have to take care to understand it.

Enumerators

Most C/C++ programmers are probably familiar with enumerators. Enumerators are often used when constant values must be combined with text. In the case of small lists, this works well and can make C# programs easier to read.

In the next example, you learn how enumerators can be implemented. The target of the example is to see how the days of a week can be processed:

```csharp
using System;

class    Demo
{
        public enum Days: byte
        {
                monday, tuesday, wednesday, thursday,
                friday, saturday, sunday
        }

        public static void Main()
        {
                Days MyDay;
                Array DayArray = Enum.GetValues(typeof(Demo.Days));
                foreach (Days Day in DayArray)
                {
                        Console.WriteLine(Day + " = "
                                + Day.ToString("d"));
                }
        }
}
```

Inside the class, we define an enumerator that's derived from `byte`. Inside the `Main` function, we define a variable that has the same data type, and we define an array that contains the values of the enumerator. For that purpose, we use the `GetValues` method. Finally, we process all values one after the other and display a string on screen. The output looks like this:

```
[hs@duron mono]$ mono ex.exe
monday = 0
tuesday = 1
wednesday = 2
thursday = 3
friday = 4
saturday = 5
sunday = 6
```

Mono displays the names of the days plus the various numbers. All together we have stored seven values.

The C# Compiler

After that introduction to C# and object orientation in general, it's time to see how C# projects can be compiled. In this section, you learn how to compile more than just one file and how various classes can be combined.

Compiling

Before you see how compiling works, we'll guide you through the steps of the compilation process itself.

The first thing to do is to call the lexer, which prepares tokens for the *parser*. In the case of Mono, the parser is based on Jay, a Java-based Berkley Port of Yacc. Miguel de Icaza ported Jay to C#. *Tokens* are code fragments that the system needs for checking the syntax. The syntax check is performed by a parser.

After creating a parse tree, the system starts to look for parent classes and tries to find out more about the meaning of the code. Before this step, the system knows about the code but it does not know what it means yet. A semantic analysis of the data leads to the final code. Therefore, Mono uses the `System.Reflection.Emit` API.

Compiling More Than Just One File

Compiling a set of files is slightly more complex than compiling just one piece of code. Huge projects are usually not implemented in one file. Therefore, it makes sense to combine multiple source files in one project and to compile the entire code with just one step.

This section teaches you the most basic fundamentals.

To see how things work, we start with an example consisting of just two files. Let's have a look at human.cs:

```
using System;

public class     Human
{
        public Human()
        {
                Console.WriteLine("a child without name ...");
        }

        public Human(string name)
        {
                Console.WriteLine(name + " is born ...");
        }
}
```

Now let's see what we can find in main.cs:

```
class    Demo
{
        public static void Main()
        {
                Human paul = new Human();
                Human hugo = new Human("Hugo");
        }
}
```

If we have a closer look at those two files, we'll find out that we include only Human—the System namespace isn't included because we need it inside our classes anyway.

To compile the code, we can use the following command:

```
[hs@duron mono]$ mcs /optimize main.cs human.cs /out:human.exe
Compilation succeeded
```

Just list all files in a single command line. To define which file to create, just use /out:. Older versions of Mono supported the -o flag as well, but we recommend using the newer syntax. In our case, the output is sent to human.exe. With the help of /optimize, we tell the C# compiler to optimize the output.

As you can see in the listing, the output can be called just like always:

```
[hs@duron mono]$ mono human.exe
a child without name ...
Hugo is born ...
```

In this example, the entire code has been transformed to one big EXE file. However, it's often useful to compile objects as separate modules. This is no problem for the C# compiler. In the case of Mono, DLL files are used. To generate a DLL, just do as we've done in the following listing:

```
[hs@duron mono]$ mcs --target library /out:human.dll human.cs
Compilation succeeded
```

Now that the DLL has been created, we can take it and compile the main program;

```
[hs@duron mono]$ mcs -L . -reference:human.dll ex.cs
Compilation succeeded
```

The process will lead to the desired result:

```
[hs@duron mono]$ mono ex.exe
a child without name ...
Hugo is born ...
```

The more complex your application, the more important it is to make use of modules and DLL files.

Compiler Flags

In this section, we deal with the most important flags of the C# compiler. The syntax of mcs is comparatively simple:

```
mcs [option] [source-files]
```

The next section contains an overview of the parameters supported by mcs:

```
[hs@duron mono]$ mcs --help
Mono C# compiler, (C) 2001 Ximian, Inc.
mcs [options] source-files
   --about           About the Mono C# compiler
   -checked[+|-]     Set default context to checked
   -codepage:ID      Sets code page to the one in ID
                     (number, 'utf8' or 'reset')
   -define:S1[;S2]   Defines one or more symbols (short: /d:)
   -debug[+-]        Generate debugging information
   -g                Generate debugging information
   --fatal           Makes errors fatal
   -lib:PATH1,PATH2  Adds the paths to the assembly link path
   -main:class       Specified the class that contains the entry point
   -noconfig[+|-]    Disables implicit references to assemblies
   -nostdlib[+|-]    Does not load core libraries
```

```
    -nowarn:W1[,W2]      Disables one or more warnings
    -out:FNAME           Specifies output file
    --parse              Only parses the source file
    --expect-error X     Expect that error X will be encountered
    -recurse:SPEC        Recursively compiles the files in SPEC ([dir]/file)
    -reference:ASS       References the specified assembly (-r:ASS)
    --stacktrace         Shows stack trace at error location
    -target:KIND         Specifies the target (KIND is one of: exe, winexe,
                         library, module), (short: /t:)
    --timestamp          Displays time stamps of various compiler events
    -unsafe[+¦-]         Allows unsafe code
    -warnaserror[+¦-]    Treat warnings as errors
    -warn:LEVEL          Sets warning level (the highest is 4, the default)
    -v                   Verbose parsing (for debugging the parser)

Resources:
    -linkresource:FILE[,ID] Links FILE as a resource
    -resource:FILE[,ID]     Embed FILE as a resource
    --mcs-debug X        Sets MCS debugging level to X
    @file                Read response file for more options

Options can be of the form -option or /option
```

The listing was generated with the help of mcs 0.23. As you can see in the last line, the compiler supports Unix and .NET-style options. However, we recommend sticking to the .NET-compliant options.

In Brief

- C# is one of the most flexible programming languages.

- C# provides a rich set of data types.

- Arrays can be used to store sets of information.

- Loops can be used to repeat various steps.

- Variables can be seen inside a block.

- Namespaces help the programmer build logical blocks containing certain variables.

- The C# compiler enables you to compile more than just one file.

Exception Handling and Debugging

Managing exceptions and errors in general is so fundamental that we've decided to dedicate an entire chapter to them.

The central mechanism for managing problems is an *exception*. With the help of exceptions, the way software works can be defined precisely and to handle errors.

Exception Handling

Let's start our tour through the world of errors and problems. C# provides simple methods to deal with errors. In this section, we take a closer look at the most important mechanisms.

try/catch

try and catch are the most important keywords you can use for handling errors. The advantage of C#'s way of handling errors is that more than just one problem can be caught at once. In C#, every function needs its own code for handling exceptions properly. It's comparatively hard to check entire blocks for errors. Although code fragments can be packed into functions, the problem is still there.

try and catch make many things significantly easier. Before we discuss the details, let's look at a basic example:

```
using System;

class    Demo
{
```

```
public static void Main()
{
        int i = 2, j = 0;
        double result;

        result = i / j;
        Console.WriteLine("Result: " + result);
    }
}
```

We try to perform a division by 0, but this leads to a runtime error:

```
[hs@duron exception]$ mono main.exe

** (process:11991): WARNING **: unhandled exception
System.DivideByZeroException: "Division by zero"
in <0x00017> .Demo:Main ()
```

The program terminates unexpectedly. Obviously, this isn't the desired behavior of our program. To handle the exception properly, we have to use try and catch. The following piece of code presents a simple solution for our problem:

```
using System;

class   Demo
{
        public static void Main()
        {
                int i = 2, j = 0;
                double result;

                try
                {
                        result = i / j;
                        Console.WriteLine("Result: " + result);
                }
                catch
                {
                        Console.WriteLine("Wrong division ...");
                }
        }
}
```

The code we want to check is inside the try block. If an error arises, the catch block is called. In this case, some text is displayed on screen:

```
[hs@duron exception]$ mono main.exe
Wrong division ...
```

Whenever an error occurs, an object is returned. That object is usually an exception. The type of this error can be chosen explicitly. However, in this example, we use the default object.

Let's get to the next example:

```
using System;

class    Demo
{
        public static void Main()
        {
                double result;
                try
                {
                        result = 2.0 / 0;
                        Console.WriteLine("Result: " + result);
                }
                catch    (Exception e)
                {
                        Console.WriteLine("Error: " + e.Message);
                }
        }
}
```

Here, a correct error message is displayed. As you can see, this can be done easily by using a method called Message.

Let's have a look at an additional example that's pretty similar. The code you just saw contains a division by zero, but in this case the result is different:

```
[hs@duron exception]$ mono main.exe
Result: Infinity
```

Infinity happens when an invalid division is performed. Infinite values are important, and it's necessary to know how C# performs under these circumstances.

finally

In various situations, it might be useful to perform some action no matter what a certain block does. For that purpose, C# provides the keyword finally. The system makes sure that this block is always executed—even when an error occurs. The following example tries to make this a bit clearer:

```csharp
using System;

class   Demo
{
        public static void Main()
        {
                int i = 2, j = 0;
                double result;

                try
                {
                        result = i / j;
                }
                catch ( DivideByZeroException e )
                {
                        Console.WriteLine("Error: " + e.Message );
                }
                finally
                {
                        Console.WriteLine("This is the end");
                }
        }
}
```

The try block raises an error because we try to perform a division by zero. The code catches the error with the help of the DivideByZeroException object. After detecting the problem, the finally block is called and an additional message is displayed on screen. When you run the program, the result will look like this:

```
[hs@duron mono]$ mono prog.exe
Error: Division by zero
This is the end
```

Classes for Managing Errors

C# provides a rich set of classes for managing errors. As we're writing this book, Mono does not yet provide a full set of classes, but things are changing rapidly. In this section, we look at the most important classes provided by the Mono framework:

- AppDomainUnloadedException: Returned when somebody tries to access an application domain that has not been loaded yet.

- ApplicationException: A nonfatal error has occurred.

- ArgumentException: Returned when an argument of a class is invalid.

- ArgumentNullException: Returned when a Null reference is passed to a function.

- ArgumentOutOfRangeException: Returned when an argument is out of range.

- ArithmeticException: A calculation or a conversion has reported an error.

- ArrayTypeMismatchException: Returned when a variable with the wrong data type is assigned to an array.

- BadImageFormatException: Occurs in case of a broken DLL.

- CannotUnloadAppDomainException: A module cannot be unloaded.

- ContextMarshalException: Returned when it's impossible to arrange an object across boundaries.

- DivideByZeroException: Division by zero.

- DllNotFoundException: A DLL has not been found.

- DuplicateWaitObjectException: Thrown when an object occurs in a synchronization object more than once.

- EntryPointNotFoundException: Happens when the Main function cannot be called.

- Exception: The default class for managing errors.

- ExecutionEngineException: An error in the common language runtime has occurred.

- FieldAccessException: Returned when somebody tries to access data that is protected with private or protected.

- FormatException: A format does not fit to an argument.

- IndexOutOfRangeException: Thrown when somebody tries to access a position in a field that does not exist.

- InvalidOperationException: Happens when a method is not suitable for the current state of an array.

- InvalidProgramException: In most cases, this error shows an error in the compiler suite.

- MemberAccessException: Thrown when a member of a class cannot be accessed.

- MethodAccessException: Thrown when a method cannot be called.

- MissingFieldException: A field cannot be accessed.

- MissingMemberException: Somebody tried to access a member of a class that does not exist.

- MissingMethodException: Happens when a nonexistent method is called.

- MulticastNotSupportedException: Returned when somebody tries to combine two objects that cannot be combined.

- NotFiniteNumberException: Marks a positive or a negative infinite number. (NaN means *not a number.*)

- NotImplementedException: Happens when a method has not been implemented yet.

- NotSupportedException: A request is not supported (for example, data is sent to a stream that does not exist).

- NullReferenceException: A reference to Null is dereferenced.

- OutOfMemoryException: Not enough memory is available.

- OverflowException: An overflow has occurred.

- PlatformNotSupportedException: A function call is not accepted by a certain platform.

- RankException: Returned when an array with a wrong number of dimensions is passed to a method.

- StackOverflowException: An overflow has occurred on the stack. This might happen when there are too many pending requests on the system. Currently, Mono core dumps and does not catch this error.

- SystemException: Contains an error thrown by the system.

- TypeInitializationException: Error while initializing.

- TypeLoadException: A type cannot be loaded correctly.

- TypeUnloadException: A type cannot be unloaded correctly.

- UnauthorizedAccessException: Marks I/O problems as well as security restrictions.

- UriFormatException: An incorrect URL has been found.

If you want to know which errors have already been implemented for your version of Mono, we recommend reading mono/mcs-X.XX/class/corlib/System.

In that directory, you'll find all relevant information and all code fragments that are related to the System namespace in general.

checked **and** unchecked

C# provides a mechanism that tries to find out whether an operation has lead to an overflow. This is truly important when it comes to complex mathematical operations.

With the help of the keywords checked and unchecked, you can define the behavior when it comes to an overflow.

Let's check out some code and see what happens:

```
using System;

class    Demo
{
        public static void Main()
        {
                int a, b;
                int result;
                a = b = 300000;
                try
                {
                        checked
                        {
                                result = a * b;
                        }
                }
                catch    (OverflowException e)
                {
                        Console.WriteLine("Overflow: " + e.Message);
                }

        }
}
```

We multiply two values with each other. The result is a huge number that leads to an overflow. To get rid of the overflow, we use the checked keyword and a try block. With the help of catch, it's an easy task to detect the problem.

The exact opposite of checked is unchecked. In a few cases, it might be useful not to check for overflows. The following listing contains an example of such a situation:

```
using System;

class    Demo
{
        public static void Main()
        {
                int a, b;
                int random;
                a = b = 123456789;
                try
                {
                        unchecked
                        {
                                random = a * b;
                                Console.WriteLine("Random: " + random);
                        }
                }
                catch    (OverflowException e)
                {
                        Console.WriteLine("Overflow: " + e.Message);
                }

        }
}
```

Although we caused an overflow, it isn't reported and does not occur. The preceding example
shows a trivial deterministic random generator. The words *deterministic* and *random generator*
might look strange in this context, but in the case of scientific applications, deterministic
random generators are important because they help you generate a certain result again and
again. In our case, the random value is an integer variable. However, it is also possible to
create lower random numbers by using modulo operations.

Debugging

Debugging C# applications based on the Mono framework is not that trivial. It takes a huge
knowledge base to handle Mono properly and to hunt down bugs efficiently.

In this section, we focus on debugging in general and you'll learn about the basic steps in the
process.

JIT

For debugging a C# application, you'll have to run the just-in-time (JIT) compiler inside a debugger. On Linux systems, the GDB (GNU Debugger) is widespread. It provides all relevant mechanisms for debugging an application. Before you can use the debugger, you need a file containing information about all data types and so forth. This file has to be regenerated every time a method is compiled.

Using the JIT compiler is comparatively complex. Therefore, we won't deal with the details because they're far beyond the scope of this book. It's certain that, in the near future, there will be more comfortable methods that are optimized for Mono and C#, such as the debugger by Martin Baulig.

Working with the `Main` Function

A comfortable way to debug is to use more than just one `Main` function. On first sight, this looks strange but it truly is comfortable. In this section, you'll learn how you can make use of more than just one `Main` function.

Let's get started with a look at an example:

```
using System;

class    Demo
{
        public static void Main()
        {
                Console.WriteLine("Main ...");
        }
}

class    Demo_Debug
{
        public static void Main()
        {
                Console.WriteLine("Debugging Code ...");
        }
}
```

In this case, you can see two classes. Each of those classes has one `Main` function. When developing an application, the second `Main` function can be used for debugging purposes. The first `Main` function can be utilized to turn off the debugging mode.

As you can see in the next listing, the compiler reports an error:

```
[hs@duron mono]$ mcs main.cs
main.cs(5) error CS0017: Program 'main.exe'  has more than one
entry point defined: 'Demo.Main()'
main.cs(13) error CS0017: Program 'main.exe'  has more than
one entry point defined: 'Demo_Debug.Main()'
Compilation failed: 2 error(s), 0 warnings
```

Mono cannot find out which class should be used as a starting point. This information must be passed to the system.

The following listing shows how you can tell Mono which entry point to use:

```
[hs@duron csharp]$ mcs /main:Demo main.cs
Compilation succeeded
```

In this case, we'll use the Demo class. Let's see what comes out:

```
[hs@duron csharp]$ mono main.exe
Debugging Code ...
```

The program is ready for action.

In Brief

- try/catch is the most popular mechanism for managing exceptions.

- Exceptions are an essential task for every programmer.

- finally makes sure that C# provides certain operations no matter what else might happen.

- Unfortunately, Mono does not yet provide a working compiler.

- Running the JIT with a debugger is a complex task.

- With the help of multiple main functions, it's possible to tell the program how to start.

Classes, Inheritance, and Polymorphism

5

Objects are a core component of the object-oriented programming (OOP) paradigm. Objects help the programmer to split a program into logical blocks that can be accessed via predefined interfaces. The way that an object works should not be seen by the user. The advantage of that is that a user does not have to know about the details of an implementation. This significantly reduces the complexity of a problem. The greater the complexity of a program, the more it benefits from the advantages of OOP. Especially when many different people are working on one piece of software, you'll soon find the advantages of object orientation.

In this section, you see how objects can be used with Mono and C#.

Classes

Objects are the key component of an object-oriented language. In previous chapters, we used objects without taking a closer look at the concepts the system is built on. In this example, it's time to look at some advanced technologies, and you'll see how the efficiency of software can be raised even more.

Overloading Methods

Overloading objects is an old concept and it is used with most modern programming languages. The basic idea of overloading is that a method can be available in many different versions, and it can accept different parameter lists. That way, one name can be associated with a very special operation, and the correct name can easily be assigned to it. To make this theoretical overview a bit clearer, we decided to include a basic example that shows the main ideas of function overloading:

```
using System;

class   Demo
{
        public static void Main()
        {
                Human paul = new Human();
                Human hugo = new Human("Hugo");
        }
}

public class    Human
{
        public Human()
        {
                Console.WriteLine("a child without name ...");
        }

        public Human(string name)
        {
                Console.WriteLine(name + " is born ...");
        }
}
```

In our case, the class consists of two constructors. The first constructor does not accept parameters, but the second constructor accepts a string that defines the name of the person we're creating. Depending on the parameters you're using, Mono finds the right function and the corresponding code is called. In that way, it's possible to write functions whose behavior depends on the list of parameters.

Let's see which output is generated if the program is compiled and executed:

```
[hs@duron mono]$ mono main.exe
a child without name ...
Hugo is born ...
```

Two different constructors are called.

Overloading methods has many advantages, but it's also dangerous because the effort required to find an error grows. In some cases, it's hard to find out which parameters are used and which functions are called. You will have this problem more often than you might think. Sometimes it's necessary to call a function with an undefined number of parameters. C# and the Mono framework provide solutions to that problem. In the next example, you can see how the average value of a variable number of values could be computed:

```
using System;

public class Demo
{
        public static void Main()
        {
                Series r = new Series(1, 2, 3, 4);
                Console.WriteLine("Result: " + r.avg);
        }
}


public class Series
{
        public double avg;

        public Series(params int[] zahl)
        {
                double Sum = 0;
                for     (int i = 0; i < zahl.Length; i++)
                {
                        Sum += zahl[i];
                }

                avg = Sum / zahl.Length;
        }
}
```

We implement a class that we can use to compute the average of a list of values. The number of parameters accepted by this method is more or less unlimited. The important thing is that the keyword params has to be used; otherwise, C# does not know what to do because it thinks that just one parameter is being sent to the method you're about to call.

The next listing shows what the result will look like:

```
[hs@duron mono]$ mono main.exe
Result: 2.5
```

When working with a variable set of parameters, you must not forget to put the variable parameter list at the end. Otherwise, Mono cannot find out which parameter is part of a certain list.

Overloading Operators

With the help of a modern OOP language, it's possible to overload operators. The advantage of that is that you need not invent a name for a certain method of an object—all you have to do is to define an operator that has the desired behavior. Overloading an object is not difficult and it makes many things much easier and helps make your code more readable.

Operators are strongly related to data types, and that's exactly what we want to deal with in this section. The way complex numbers are handled is a standard example for modern object-oriented development that's discussed in many books dealing with the subject. In the next example, you learn how complex numbers can be implemented in C#:

```
using System;

class Complex
{
        private int x;
        private int y;

        // Constructor
        public Complex()
        {
        }

        // Constructor + Initialization
        public Complex(int i, int j)
        {
                x = i;
                y = j;
        }

        // Displaying data
        public void PrintComplex()
        {
                Console.WriteLine("{0} + {1}i", x, y);
        }

        // Implementation of the + operator
        public static Complex operator+(Complex number1,Complex number2)
```

```
        {
                Complex temp = new Complex();
                temp.x = number1.x + number2.x;
                temp.y = number1.y + number2.y;
                return temp;
        }
}

class Demo
{
        public static void Main()
        {
                Complex number1 = new Complex(10, 20);
                Complex number2 = new Complex(20, 30);
                Complex ergebnis = new Complex();

                ergebnis = number1 + number2;
                ergebnis.PrintComplex();
        }
}
```

Our program consists of two classes. The class called `Complex` contains the implementation of the object we'll need later in the `Main` function. The complex `Class` contains two variables. One of these is for the real part of the number and one for the complex part. Two constructors are provided: The first one creates an empty number, and the second one creates and initializes the number. The `PrintComplex` method is an additional important part—it can be used for displaying the content of the object. Because we don't want to use a method all the time, we define the + operator. This makes the code easier to understand and much more readable. In our case, the + operator does nothing other than perform two simple additions. The return values of the + operator is a complex number as well.

When we execute the program, we see one line:

```
[hs@duron mono]$ mono main.exe
30 + 50i
```

Overloading operators is truly simple and has many advantages, but there are also some major restrictions programmers have to face: Some operators cannot be overloaded for several reasons. In the next line, you can see a list of all operators that are not suitable for listing operation overloading:

`., &&, sizeof, checked, f(), ¦¦, typeof, unchecked, [], ?:, as, ->, =, new, is`

In addition, you have to take into consideration that as soon as certain operators are over-loaded, various additional operations are overloaded automatically. This is an important subject, and we focus on it in the next example (don't forget to include the class you saw in the previous example):

```
class Demo
{
        public static void Main()
        {
                Complex number1 = new Complex(10,20);
                Complex number2 = new Complex(20,30);
                Complex result = new Complex();

                result = number1 + number2;
                result.PrintComplex();
                result += number1;
                result.PrintComplex();
        }
}
```

The += operator is also defined. This happens automatically and you need not think about that feature anymore:

```
[hs@duron klassen]$ mono test.exe
30 + 50i
40 + 70i
```

The result meets our expectations.

Readonly

Sometimes it's necessary to define variables that cannot be overwritten anymore. To that end, C# provides the readonly keyword. Any variable that has been defined as readonly cannot be modified. This makes sense, as you can see in the next example:

```
using System;

class Operation
{
        public readonly double pi = 3.141;
        public readonly double e = 2.718;

        public Operation()
        {
```

```
                Console.WriteLine("Pi: " + pi);
                Console.WriteLine("e: " + e);
        }
}

class Demo
{
        public static void Main()
        {
                Operation x = new Operation();
        }
}
```

Inside the Operation class, two variables that should not be modified are defined. readonly significantly raises the security of an application. Let's see what comes out if we try to start the software:

```
[hs@duron klassen]$ mono test.exe
Pi: 3.141
e: 2.718
```

static

static is an important keyword when it comes to C# applications. Until now, we've used this keyword without telling you about the technical details. Therefore, it's time to have a closer look at this topic.

Static methods are not called for instances but for definitions of classes. There can never be more than one version of a static method. In contrast to ordinary methods, static methods can be used only in combination with static members of a class. In case of mathematical operations, this makes sense because it's easy to work with data that isn't part of a class. With the help of static methods, many problems can be solved easily and the number of classes in an application can be reduced. Just think of simple computations that you'll need in many different situations—you need not define a class for every single data source anymore because this would be far too confusing. Static methods can do a good job and will make your daily work easier. A static method usually accepts values, processes them, and returns them again.

To see how things work, take a look at the next example:

```
using System;

class Demo
{
```

```
        public static void Main()
        {
                Console.WriteLine(MakeAverage(3, 2));
        }

        public static double MakeAverage(double a, double b)
        {
                return (a + b) / 2;
        }
}
```

```
[hs@duron klassen]$ mono static.exe
2.5
```

If the method were not static, the compiler would report a fatal error:

```
[hs@duron klassen]$ mcs static.cs
static.cs(7) error CS0120: An object reference is required for the
non-static field 'MakeAverage'
Compilation failed: 1 error(s), 0 warnings
```

Properties

Properties are members of classes that enable us to access the data of an instance. In contrast to C++, you need not define methods to access members of a class. A simple example will explain the concept:

```
using System;

class Point
{
        int     x;
        int     y;

        public int X
        {
                get
                {
                        return x;
                }
                set
                {
                        x = value;
```

```
                }
        }

        public int Y
        {
                get
                {
                        return y;
                }
                set
                {
                        y = value;
                }
        }
}

class Demo
{
        public static void Main()
        {
                Point MyPoint = new Point();
                MyPoint.X = 10;
                MyPoint.Y = MyPoint.X + 5;
                Console.WriteLine("({0} / {1})",
                        MyPoint.X, MyPoint.Y);
        }
}
```

We implemented a class that can store points. For every variable, we implemented a set as well as a get block. The get block can be used to retrieve a value; the set block helps us to assign data to a variable. value is a magical keyword containing the value that should be assigned. As you can see in the listing, the syntax is truly simple and easy to understand, but it is still possible to modify the data being displayed by the program.

The content of a Point is displayed:

```
[hs@duron mono]$ mono main.exe
(10 / 15)
```

Delegates

Pointers to functions are a widespread feature of C and C++. However, in many cases, using pointers to functions is a good way to corrupt memory, to create core dumps, and to produce other kinds of problems. When working with pointers, the system does not crash when the actual error occurs. It happens later because of corrupted memory. Delegates are Mono and C#'s answer to the problem. To a large extent, delegates are the same as pointers to functions in C++ (just think of typed function pointers), but there are some significant differences that a programmer must be aware of to write perfectly performing applications.

In this section, you learn how delegates can be used in C#. Let's get started with some code:

```
using System;

public delegate void MyDelegate(string input);

class Class1
{
        public void delegateMethod1(string input)
        {
                Console.WriteLine("delegateMethod1: {0}", input);
        }

        public void delegateMethod2(string input)
        {
                Console.WriteLine("delegateMethod2: {0}", input);
        }
}

class Class2
{
        public MyDelegate neuDelegate()
        {
                Class1 c2 = new Class1();
                MyDelegate d1 = new MyDelegate(c2.delegateMethod1);
                MyDelegate d2 = new MyDelegate(c2.delegateMethod2);
                MyDelegate d3 = d1 + d2;
                return d3;
        }
}

class Class3
{
        public void callDelegate(MyDelegate d, string input)
        {
                d(input);
        }
```

```
        }

class Driver
{
        static void Main(string[] args)
        {
                Class2 c2 = new Class2();
                MyDelegate d = c2.neuDelegate();
                Class3 c3 = new Class3();
                c3.callDelegate(d, "Calling the delegate");
        }
}
```

All together, our example contains four classes. The first class contains the methods we want to use as delegates. The second class defines the required delegates. As you can see, we pass a method to every delegate. In the third class, the delegates are called. The Main function can be found in the fourth class. In this example, we called this class Driver. In the next listing, you can see the output that's displayed on screen:

```
[hs@duron mono]$ mono main.exe
delegateMethod1: Calling the delegate
delegateMethod2: Calling the delegate
```

Delegates are essential, especially when a programmer has to deal with GUI programming (implementing user interfaces). In Chapter 15, "User Interfaces," which covers GUI programming, we'll get back to delegates.

Creating and Managing Namespaces

In Chapter 3, we dealt with the fundamentals of namespaces. In this section, it's time to look at some practical examples in which you can see how people can work with namespaces.

The next example consists of two parts. The first part contains a namespace including two classes. This part is in a file called namespace.cs:

```
namespace Human
{
        using System;

        public class Worker
        {
                public Worker()
                {
                        Console.WriteLine("I am a worker");
```

```
              }
      }

      public class Student
      {
              public Student()
              {
                      Console.WriteLine("I am a student");
              }
      }
}
```

Let's have a look at the code in `main.cs`:

```
using System;
using Human;

public class Demo
{
      public static void Main()
      {
              Human.Worker hugo = new Human.Worker();
              Human.Student paul = new Human.Student();
      }
}
```

Let's take a closer look at the namespace we defined. The file consists of two classes that have been combined in one namespace. To define a namespace, you have to use the predefined keyword namespace as well as a name and parenthesis. Inside the Main program, we can include the namespace with the help of the using keyword. You already know this approach because we've already used the System namespace frequently.

Inside the Main function, we define two instances. The name of the namespace can be omitted as well because we use using Mensch. It's useful to mention the namespace in the program, but it isn't mandatory. Doing so has the advantage that there can be many classes with the same name that are situated in different namespaces.

Let's see which result you can expect:

```
[hs@duron mono]$ mcs namespace.cs main.cs -o prog.exe
Compilation succeeded
[hs@duron mono]$ mono prog.exe
I am a worker
I am a student
```

As we already mentioned, it's possible to combine classes having the same name in a namespace. This concept is fundamental; therefore, we've included a second example to show how things work. In this example, we use two namespaces. Each of them contains a class called Human:

```
using System;

namespace Taxcollector
{
        public class Human
        {
                public Human()
                {
                        Console.WriteLine("You must pay taxes");
                }
        }
}

namespace Biology
{
        public class Human
        {
                public Human()
                {
                        Console.WriteLine("Humans are monkeys");
                }
        }
}
```

Inside the Main function, we create two instances of the Human object:

```
using System;
using Taxcollector;
using Science = Biology;

public class Demo
{
        public static void Main()
        {
                Taxcollector.Human hugo = new Taxcollector.Human();
                Science.Human paul = new Science.Human();
        }
}
```

As you can see in the example, it's possible to assign an alternative name to a namespace. This has many advantages because it's possible to replace complicated names with simpler ones. If you're using aliases and implementing your applications cleverly, the name of the namespace often need not be mentioned more than once. This significantly reduces the effort needed to maintain a piece of software.

As always, we tested the example:

```
[hs@localhost mono]$ mono prog.exe
You must pay taxes
Humans are monkeys
```

As you can see, C# accesses the correct constructor every time an instance is created.

Accessing Multiple Values

If you try to access the data of an instance, you'll find out that it's fairly easy to access one variable. This makes the code long and a bit ugly to read. To get rid of this problem, we want to introduce a technology that can save you a lot of work.

In the next example, you can see how many variables can be extracted at once:

```
using System;

public class Demo
{
        public static void Main()
        {
                int a = 0, b = 0;
                string c = "f";

                Human hugo = new Human(22, 178, "m");
                hugo.GetValues(ref a, ref b, ref c);

                Console.WriteLine("a: {0}, b: {1}, c: {2}", a, b, c);
        }
}

public class Human
{
        public int age;
        public int height;
        public string gender;
```

```
public Human(int age, int height, string gender)
{
        this.age = age;
        this.height = height;
        this.gender = gender;
}

public void GetValues(ref int age,
        ref int height, ref string gender)
{
        age = this.age;
        height = this.height;
        gender = this.gender;
}
}
```

The class Human is supposed to store three variables. To initialize an instance, we pass three parameters to the constructor, which are instantly assigned to the current instance.

Reading all values at once is done by a separate method. Three references are passed to this method. That way, all records can be extracted at once because all the work is done by the function. At first sight, this seems a bit complicated, but it saves some code in the case of more complex applications.

Let's see which result we can expect:

```
[hs@localhost mono]$ mono main.exe
a: 22, b: 178, c: m
```

You can see that values are assigned correctly.

Analyzing Objects

Every variable that's used inside the Mono framework is based on a data type and, respectively, an object. C# provides some interesting features for analyzing objects. In many cases, this is essential for steering an application.

Let's examine some code and see what C# provides:

```
using System;

public class Demo
{
        public static void Main()
        {
```

```
            Type aType = typeof(int);
            Console.WriteLine("int: " + aType.ToString() );

            Human Paul = new Human();
            Type PType = typeof(Human);
            Console.WriteLine("Human: " + PType.ToString() );
        }
}


public class Human
{
        public Human()
        {
        }
}
```

We pass the data type to typeof. The return type of the function is Type. To display the content of a variable, we can use the ToString method.

The following listing is displayed:

```
[hs@localhost mono]$ mono main.exe
int: System.Int32
Human: Human
```

Type provides a rich set of features. The next example tries to illustrate those features, and you'll see a list of the most important members of the class:

```
using System;

public class Demo
{
        public static void Main()
        {
                Type aType = typeof(int);

                Console.WriteLine("Assembly: " + aType.Assembly );
                Console.WriteLine("AssemblyQualifiedName: "
                        + aType.AssemblyQualifiedName );
                Console.WriteLine("Attributes: " + aType.Attributes );
                Console.WriteLine("BaseType: " + aType.BaseType );
                Console.WriteLine("DeclaringType: "
                        + aType.DeclaringType );
                Console.WriteLine("GUID: " + aType.GUID );
```

```
Console.WriteLine("HasElementType: "
        + aType.HasElementType );
Console.WriteLine("IsAbstract: " + aType.IsAbstract );
Console.WriteLine("IsAnsiClass: "
        + aType.IsAnsiClass );
Console.WriteLine("IsArray: " + aType.IsArray );
Console.WriteLine("IsAutoClass: "
        + aType.IsAutoClass );
Console.WriteLine("IsAutoLayout: "
        + aType.IsAutoLayout );
Console.WriteLine("IsByRef: " + aType.IsByRef );
Console.WriteLine("IsCOMObject: "
        + aType.IsCOMObject );
Console.WriteLine("IsEnum: " + aType.IsEnum );
Console.WriteLine("IsExplicitLayout: "
        + aType.IsExplicitLayout );
Console.WriteLine("IsImport: " + aType.IsImport );
Console.WriteLine("IsInterface: "
        + aType.IsInterface );
Console.WriteLine("IsLayoutSequential: "
        + aType.IsLayoutSequential );
Console.WriteLine("IsMarshalByRef: "
        + aType.IsMarshalByRef );
Console.WriteLine("IsNestedAssembly: "
        + aType.IsNestedAssembly );
Console.WriteLine("IsNestedFamANDAssem: "
        + aType.IsNestedFamANDAssem );
Console.WriteLine("IsNestedFamily: "
        + aType.IsNestedFamily );
Console.WriteLine("IsNestedFamORAssem: "
        + aType.IsNestedFamORAssem );
Console.WriteLine("IsNestedPrivate: "
        + aType.IsNestedPrivate );
Console.WriteLine("IsNestedPublic: "
        + aType.IsNestedPublic );
Console.WriteLine("IsNotPublic: "
        + aType.IsNotPublic );
Console.WriteLine("IsPointer: " + aType.IsPointer );
Console.WriteLine("IsPrimitive: "
        + aType.IsPrimitive );
Console.WriteLine("IsPublic: " + aType.IsPublic );
Console.WriteLine("IsSealed: " + aType.IsSealed );
```

```
                    Console.WriteLine("IsSerializable: "
                            + aType.IsSerializable );
                    Console.WriteLine("IsSpecialName: "
                            + aType.IsSpecialName );
                    Console.WriteLine("IsUnicodeClass: "
                            + aType.IsUnicodeClass );
                    Console.WriteLine("IsValueType: "
                            + aType.IsValueType );
                    Console.WriteLine("MemberType: " + aType.MemberType );
                    Console.WriteLine("Module: " + aType.Module );
                    Console.WriteLine("Name: " + aType.Name );
                    Console.WriteLine("Namespace: " + aType.Namespace );
                    Console.WriteLine("ReflectedType: "
                            + aType.ReflectedType );
                    Console.WriteLine("TypeHandle: " + aType.TypeHandle );
                    // Console.WriteLine("TypeInitializer: "
                    //      + aType.TypeInitializer );
                    Console.WriteLine("UnderlyingSystemType: "
                            + aType.UnderlyingSystemType );
        }
}
```

The data type contains a rich set of variables that you can use for many purposes. Especially for complex data types, the information provided by the Type class is essential.

The following listing contains some information about the integer data type:

```
[hs@localhost mono]$ mono main.exe
Assembly: mscorlib
AssemblyQualifiedName: System.Int32, mscorlib
Attributes: Public, SequentialLayout, Sealed, Serializable, BeforeFieldInit
BaseType: System.ValueType
DeclaringType:
GUID: 00000000-0000-0000-0000-000000000000
HasElementType: False
IsAbstract: False
IsAnsiClass: True
IsArray: False
IsAutoClass: False
IsAutoLayout: False
IsByRef: False
IsCOMObject: False
IsEnum: False
```

```
IsExplicitLayout: False
IsImport: False
IsInterface: False
IsLayoutSequential: True
IsMarshalByRef: False
IsNestedAssembly: False
IsNestedFamANDAssem: False
IsNestedFamily: False
IsNestedFamORAssem: False
IsNestedPrivate: False
IsNestedPublic: False
IsNotPublic: False
IsPointer: False
IsPrimitive: True
IsPublic: True
IsSealed: True
IsSerializable: True
IsSpecialName: False
IsUnicodeClass: False
IsValueType: True
MemberType: TypeInfo
Module: Reflection.Module: /usr/lib/corlib.dll
Name: Int32
Namespace: System
ReflectedType:
TypeHandle: System.RuntimeTypeHandle
UnderlyingSystemType: System.Int32
```

Most of the information displayed here isn't used too often, but some variables will be needed frequently.

MethodInfo

When analyzing objects, it just isn't enough to look at the properties of an object. It's important to know which methods a certain class provides. Therefore, you can use the System. Reflection namespace. In the example, you can see how the GetMethods method can be called to find out which methods the int class provides:

```
using System;
using System.Reflection;

public class Demo
{
```

```
public static void Main()
{
        Type aType = typeof(int);
        MethodInfo[] methods = aType.GetMethods();

        foreach (MethodInfo m in methods)
        {
                Console.WriteLine("m: " + m);
        }
}
}
```

We use an object called aType to retrieve a list of the desired methods. The result is an instance of the MethodInfo object. The content of the array can be displayed with the help of a loop.

The result will look like this:

```
[hs@duron klassen]$ mono main.exe
m: Boolean ReferenceEquals(Object, Object)
m: String ToString()
m: Type GetType()
m: Int32 GetHashCode()
m: Boolean Equals(Object, Object)
m: Boolean Equals(Object)
m: String ToString()
m: Int32 GetHashCode()
m: Boolean Equals(Object)
m: TypeCode GetTypeCode()
m: String ToString(String, IFormatProvider)
m: String ToString(String)
m: String ToString(IFormatProvider)
m: String ToString()
m: Int32 Parse(String, NumberStyles, IFormatProvider)
m: Int32 Parse(String, NumberStyles)
m: Int32 Parse(String, IFormatProvider)
m: Int32 Parse(String)
m: Int32 GetHashCode()
m: Boolean Equals(Object)
m: Int32 CompareTo(Object)
```

As you can see, integer values are powerful and provide most of the methods you need to build efficient applications.

MemberInfo

Extracting a list of members works pretty much like extracting methods:

```
using System;
using System.Reflection;

public class Demo
{
        public static void Main()
        {
                Type aType = typeof(int);
                MemberInfo[] member = aType.GetMembers();

                foreach (MemberInfo m in member)
                {
                        Console.WriteLine("m: " + m);
                }
        }
}
```

The version of Mono this book is based on does not support the required feature yet, so the system reports a runtime error:

```
[hs@duron klassen]$ mono main.exe

Unhandled Exception: System.NotImplementedException: The requested
feature is not yet implemented
in <0x0002b> 00 System.MonoType:GetMembers
(System.Reflection.BindingFlags)
in <0x00043> 00 .Demo:Main ()
```

Inheritance

Every modern object-oriented language supports inheritance. Inheritance is a powerful feature that can help you to build even more powerful applications.

In this section, we take a close look at the fundamental concepts of inheritance, and you learn where to use inheritance efficiently.

Basic Concepts

Classes provide certain methods and have a set of properties. When it comes to inheritance, the features of a class are inherited by child classes, which means that a child class will have all features of its parent class plus some proprietary information. In addition, a class can redefine a feature of the parent class. To make this concept clearer, let's look at a simple example: Imagine a class that can be used to store geometric objects. A geometric object has properties such as color and circumference. However, there are also special geometric objects such as points, rectangles, and circles. This kind of object can be implemented as a derived class that inherits all properties from the parent class. Inheritance saves a lot of code because some features need not be implemented for every class—classes can inherit from a parent class. In the case of complex object hierarchies, this has many advantages.

Simple Examples

After that first theoretical overview, let's look at a simple yet practical example:

```
using System;

public class GeometricObject
{
        string  Color;

        public GeometricObject()
        {
        }

        public GeometricObject(string a)
        {
                Color = a;
        }

        public void Desc()
        {
                Console.WriteLine("Color: " + Color + "\n");
        }
}

public class Point : GeometricObject
{
        string Color;
        int     x;
        int     y;

        public Point(string a, int b, int c)
        {
```

```
                Color = a;
                x = b;
                y = c;
        }

        public void Desc()
        {
                Console.WriteLine("Color: " + Color);
                Console.WriteLine("X: " + x);
                Console.WriteLine("Y: " + y + "\n");
        }
}

class Demo
{
        public static void Main()
        {
                GeometricObject obj = new GeometricObject("blue");
                obj.Desc();

                Point pnt = new Point("red", 12, 9);
                pnt.Desc();
        }
}
```

At the beginning of the program, we implement the parent class. The parent class has exactly one property. It contains two constructors and one method for displaying the content of the instance. After the parent class, we add two subclasses. After the colon, we tell the compiler which parent class should be used. In our case, the GeometricObject object is used. The Point object has three properties and just one constructor. In addition, we define a method for displaying a description of the class.

Older versions of Mono did not report an error when compiling the program. The Microsoft compiler behaves the same way as Mono. The warning is thrown because we haven't used the keywords virtual and override:

```
[hs@localhost mono]$ mcs main.cs
main.cs(35) warning CS0108: The keyword new is required on 'Point.Desc'
because it hides inherited member 'GeometricObject.Desc'
Compilation succeeded - 1 warning(s)
```

If we want to get rid of the compiler warning, we could use the following two lines:

```
virtual public void Desc()
override public void Desc()
```

Let's see what happens if we start the program:

```
[hs@localhost mono]$ mono main.exe
Color: blue

Color: red
X: 12
Y: 9
```

As you can see, Mono always calls the right method. But what happens when the desired method isn't available in the subclass? And what does C# do when the parent class has the same properties as the subclass? Let's have a look at an additional example and see what happens:

```
using System;

public class GeometricObject
{
        public string    color;

        public string Color
        {
                set
                {
                        color = value;
                }
                get
                {
                        return "The Color is: " + color;
                }
        }

        public GeometricObject()
        {
        }

        public GeometricObject(string a)
        {
                color = a;
        }

        public void Desc()
        {
```

```
                Console.WriteLine( this.Color );
        }
}

public class Point : GeometricObject
{
        public int      x;
        public int      y;

        public Point(string a, int b, int c)
        {
                color = a;
                x = b;
                y = c;
        }
}

class Demo
{
        public static void Main()
        {
                GeometricObject obj = new GeometricObject("blue");
                obj.Desc();

                Point pnt = new Point("red", 12, 9);
                pnt.Desc();
        }
}
```

In the preceding code, we add properties to the parent class to make sure that the output is handled by the object itself—this helps us because we need not define a method for every subclass. The method called Desc is quite simple. As you can see, the keyword this is used to point to the instance itself. It's important to mention that all variables of the parent are inherited—therefore, points have a color as well. If we had defined the variable in the subclass as well, it would have been redefined.

This is an important concept. Overwriting a variable or changing the scope can lead to severe bugs that are hard to find. Therefore, you must use the keyword new. The subclass does not have a method for printing the content of the instance. Still, the method is called by the Main function. C# uses the method of the parent class instead of the method of the subclass. Remember that if the subclass contains a variable for storing the color as well, you'll be surprised as soon as you can see the result.

The following output should not be surprising:

```
[hs@localhost mono]$ mono main.exe
The Color is: blue
The Color is: red
```

As we expect, the properties of the parent class are used. Pay attention to the spelling of the names of the various variables. C# is a case-sensitive language, so make sure that you don't use the wrong spelling.

More About Inheritance

Many modern object-oriented languages provide simple methods for implementing multiple inheritance, and Mono and C# are no exceptions. *Multiple inheritance* means that a class can have more than just one parent class. In the case of complex applications, this has many advantages and can help you to reduce the code required to achieve a certain target even more. In this section, we take a closer look at multiple inheritance and see how simple applications can be implemented. The way inheritance is treated in C# is not exactly multiple inheritance. As you can see, it is rather a transitive inheritance.

The next example is about creatures. creature is the most basic description of something that is living. In our example, a creature has just one property: its name. Humans are special creatures that have additional attributes. Those attributes are not provided for basic creatures. The following listing shows a short example that describes a simple scenario:

```
using System;

public class Creature
{
        public string   Name;

        public Creature()
        {
                Console.WriteLine("Hello from Creature 1");
        }

        public Creature(string a)
        {
                Name = a;
                Console.WriteLine("Hello from Creature 2");
        }
}
```

```csharp
public class Human : Creature
{
        public int      Age;

        public Human()
        {
                Console.WriteLine("Hello from Human 1");
        }

        public Human(string a, int b)
        {
                Name = a;
                Age = b;
                Console.WriteLine("Hello from Human 2");
        }

        public void Desc()
        {
                Console.WriteLine("I am {0}", this.Name );
        }
}

public class Programmer : Human
{
        public bool     InLove;

        public Programmer()
        {
                Console.WriteLine("Hello from Programmer 1");
        }

        public Programmer(string a, int b, bool c)
        {
                Name = a;
                Age = b;
                InLove = c;
                Console.WriteLine("Hello from Programmer 2");
        }
}
class Demo
{
        public static void Main()
        {
```

```
Console.WriteLine("Here comes Hans: ");
Programmer hans = new Programmer("Hans", 24, false);

Console.WriteLine("\nHere comes Andy: ");
Human andy = new Human("Andreas", 49);
andy.Desc();
        }
    }
}
```

Every class has two constructors. To see which constructor is called, we added a
Console.WriteLine command to every constructor. The class Human provides a method for
displaying information about the instance as well. In this method, we use parentheses so that
the parameters are added to the text properly.

Inside the Main function, we create two instances and display the description of the objects.
Let's start the program:

```
[hs@localhost mono]$ mono main.exe
Here comes Hans:
Hello from Creature 1
Hello from Human 1
Hello from Programmer 2

Here comes Andy:
Hello from Creature 1
Hello from Human 2
I am Andreas
```

The constructors of the parent class are called automatically by the Mono framework. This is
important to know because it is an essential concept of inheritance. When writing complex
software, it's important to understand how inheritance works.

Abstract Classes

Abstract classes are an additional and important feature of C#. Abstract classes are classes that
do not have an implementation. Classes like that are usually found on top of an object hierarchy and are extremely important for structuring code. Using them, it's possible to quickly
develop frameworks and prototypes.

In this section, you learn to implement abstract classes. Let's get started with some code:

```
using System;

abstract public class Creature
{
```

```
        public string name;

        public Creature()
        {
                // no code
        }

        abstract public void CreateDescription();
}

public class Human : Creature
{
        public int       age;

        public Human()
        {
                Console.WriteLine("Hello from Human 1");
        }

        public Human(string a, int b)
        {
                name = a;
                age = b;
                Console.WriteLine("Hello from Human 2");
        }

        public override void CreateDescription()
        {
                Console.WriteLine("I am {0}", this.name );
        }
}

class Demo
{
        public static void Main()
        {
                Console.WriteLine("Here comes Andy: ");
                Human andy = new Human("Andreas", 49);
                andy.CreateDescription();
        }
}
```

The class Creature is implemented as abstract class. The class called Human is a subclass of Creature. Human is doing the actual work because it contains the actual implementation. When implementing derived classes, it's necessary to define the method as override rather than new because otherwise the compiler reports an error. The Main function creates an instance of the object and a description is displayed.

When starting the program, the following data is generated:

```
[hs@localhost mono]$ mono main.exe
Here comes Andy:
Hello from Human 2
I am Andreas
```

When working with abstract classes, you must know that it isn't possible to create an instance of an abstract class. When you add the following line to the program, you'll see what happens:

```
Creature paul = new Creature("Paul");
```

The compiler reports an error and complains that it cannot create an instance of the object:

```
[hs@duron klassen]$ mcs abstract.cs
prop.cs(41) error CS0144: It is not possible to create instances of
interfaces or abstract classes
Compilation failed: 1 error(s), 0 warnings
```

The parent class of all abstract classes is the object class. It is the template for all classes defined inside the Mono framework.

Disabling Inheritance

For security reasons, it might be useful to explicitly turn off inheritance. To facilitate this, Mono provides sealed classes. The following example shows how a sealed class can be implemented:

```
public sealed class Creature
{
        public string name;

        public Creature(string a)
        {
                name = a;
        }
}
```

In this case, it is not possible to define a subclass.

Polymorphism

Diversity is better than a monoculture. For everybody who believes in diversity, polymorphism might be the right thing. Polymorphism is the art of making one thing appear in many different facets and in many different ways, but what does that mean when talking about object-oriented languages? This section is entirely dedicated to polymorphism and you'll learn about the main benefits of this feature.

Imagine a set of similar instances of an object. The target of this example is to treat all instances the same way and to find the correct method for every single instance. The next example focuses on this approach:

```
using System;

// parent class ...
abstract public class Vehicle
{
        public Vehicle()
        {
        }

        public virtual void Drive()
        {
                Console.WriteLine("The vehicle moves");
        }
}


// derived class ...
public class CommercialCar : Vehicle
{
        public CommercialCar()
        {
        }

        public override void Drive()
        {
                Console.WriteLine("The commercial car moves");
        }
}

// derived class ...
public class PrivateCar : Vehicle
{
```

```
        public PrivateCar()
        {
        }

        public override void Drive()
        {
                Console.WriteLine("The private car moves");
        }
}


// main program
public class Demo
{
        public static void Main()
        {
                // Creating instances
                Vehicle[] Auto = new Vehicle[2];
                Auto[0] = new CommercialCar();
                Auto[1] = new PrivateCar();

                // driving around ...
                for     (int i = 0; i < 2; i++)
                {
                        Auto[i].Drive();
                }
        }
}
```

We implement an abstract class and two derived classes. Every derived class provides a method called Drive. In the Main function, we define an array and assign instances to every position inside the array. Pay attention to the data type of the instances we assign to the array. Every instance is different, but all instances are treated the same way inside the loop. The way we treat our data is called *polymorphism*.

When you start the program, you can see how the application behaves:

```
[hs@localhost mono]$ mono main.exe
The commercial car moves
The private car moves
```

Interfaces

Up to now, we've dealt with many features of a modern object-oriented programming language. The tools you've already seen should provide a solid base for implementing applications and for finding efficient solutions for every common problem. Still, the Mono framework and C# provide even more features than you might think. This section is dedicated to interfaces. You will need interfaces daily because they help you to structure your code.

Fundamental Concepts

To understand interfaces completely, it's necessary to see the difference between classes and interfaces. A class is a combination of variables and methods, which is used to perform operations. A method defines the behavior of an object. The behavior can be seen as the soul and the power of an object. In contrast, an interface defines typical interfaces, which means that it defines the behavior an object should have. Interfaces define the way things should be, whereas objects do the actual work.

In this chapter, you've already seen that this can also be done with the help of a parent class. The problem is that this does not always work and not every situation can be modeled with the help of parent classes. Whenever it's necessary to define structure for more than just one object hierarchy, interfaces are definitely a good choice.

To make this subject matter a bit clearer, let's look at an example: Assume that we have two class hierarchies. One hierarchy deals with animals. That hierarchy contains objects for managing animals as well as subclasses for managing cows, sheep, and so forth. The second class hierarchy contains classes for managing plants. There's also a set of subclasses, such as roses and birches. Our class hierarchies are working absolutely independently and they have nothing to do with each other. Still, it could be useful to define a set of methods that every object should have. A good example of a method that every object should have is a function that contains the content of an instance. An interface is a sort of contract that tells the programmer what to do. Interfaces can help you to make sure that nothing important is forgotten.

Mono supports interfaces as proposed by the .NET Framework. The way interfaces work in Mono and .NET is similar—at least, there are no intentional differences.

In the following section, you'll learn about interfaces and all the things that you'll need for your practical work.

Simple Interfaces

After that first theoretical overview, it's time to have a look at some practical examples. We hope that our example will help you to understand interfaces.

In the first example, we focus on the syntax of C#. We implement an interface that forces us to implement exactly one method:

```
using System;

interface IHuman
{
        void Walk();
}

class Human : IHuman
{
        public void Walk()
        {
                Console.WriteLine("Walking :)");
        }
}

public class Demo
{
        public static void Main()
        {
                Human Hugo = new Human();
                Hugo.Walk();
        }
}
```

The name of an interface usually starts with an I. This isn't a must, but a convention that everybody should accept in order to understand the code more easily. In our example, the interface makes sure that a method called Walk has been implemented. In addition, we implement a class called Human that provides exactly what the interface forces us to do. We can solve the problem with the help of inheritance because Human inherits from the interface. It is important to see that the interface is just a definition of the actual implementation.

When executing the program, you won't face any problems:

```
[hs@localhost mono]$ mono main.exe
Walking :)
```

Inherited Interfaces

In many cases, it can be useful to use inheritance in combination with interfaces—that's easily done. In the next example, we define an interface called IChild that inherits from

IHuman. The syntax does not differ from the one you just saw. We use a colon to tell the compiler who inherits what.

```csharp
using System;

interface IHuman
{
        void Walk();
}

interface IChild : IHuman
{
        void Jump();
}

class Demo : IChild
{
        public static void Main()
        {
                Demo Luke = new Demo();
                Luke.Walk();
                Luke.Jump();
        }

        public void Walk()
        {
                Console.WriteLine("The child walks");
        }

        public void Jump()
        {
                Console.WriteLine("The child jumps");
        }
}
```

In this case, the main class inherits from IChild. Inside the Main function, we create an instance of an object and access the desired methods. As you can see, it's no problem to define an instance of the main class.

Let's see what comes out when the program is started:

```
[hs@localhost mono]$ mono main.exe
The child walks
The child jumps
```

It's no problem to inherit from more than just one interface. In case of classes, this would not be possible.

Missing Methods

Interfaces define a set of methods that are essential to the program. If a class inherits from an interface, all proposed methods must be implemented because otherwise the compiler will report an error:

```
[hs@duron mono]$ mcs interface.cs
interface.cs(19) error CS0117: 'Demo' does not contain a definition for
'Springen'
interface.cs(13) error CS0536: 'Demo' does not implement interface
member 'IChild.Jump'
Compilation failed: 2 error(s), 0 warnings
```

Overloading Methods

The ability to overload methods is a key feature of every modern object-oriented language. As you have already seen in this book, it's possible to define various versions of a method, which accept different lists of parameters. Even when working with interfaces, overloading is essential. You have to keep in mind that you must define the desired overloadings in the interface—it isn't enough to define just one prototype.

Let's look at an example:

```
using System;

interface IHuman
{
        void Walk(string dest);
}

class Human : IHuman
{
        public void Walk(string dest)
        {
                Console.WriteLine("Destination: " + dest);
        }

        public void Walk()
        {
                Console.WriteLine("walking along the street");
        }
```

```
        }

public class Demo
{
        public static void Main()
        {
                Human Hugo = new Human();
                Hugo.Walk();
                Hugo.Walk("Sams Publishing");
        }
}
```

In this example, we define two versions of a method called `Walk`. One of those methods has been defined inside an interface, but this does not make a difference here.

The result is always the same:

```
[hs@localhost mono]$ mono main.exe
walking along the street
Destination: Sams Publishing
```

Working with is and as

Mono provides two keywords that can help you to use interfaces more efficiently. Let's have a look at is first: If you try to cast an object, you might face trouble. Let's assume that X can be cast to `IInterface`. The compiler will accept this operation as long as `IInterface` is a valid interface. But what happens at runtime? It could easily happen that somebody tries to execute it or this has not been implemented. The result is a `System.InvalidCastException` exception and the program terminates.

No matter what you're doing, it's impossible to execute code that isn't there. To get around the problem, you can ask an object before casting it. To perform this task, you can use is. The following piece of code shows how things work:

```
if      (X is IInterface)
{
        IInterface i = (IInterface)X;
}
```

As you can see, is can help to get rid of the problem.

Let's get to as. In general, as is a combined check and cast. The syntax works like this:

```
object = expression as type;
```

In Brief

- Classes are essential components of every modern programming language.

- *Polymorphism* means that a component behaves in a certain manner depending on the way it is called.

- With the help of inheritance, the amount of code can be reduced significantly.

- Subclasses can inherit methods from parent classes.

- Methods with the same name can have different parameter lists.

- When methods are missing inside a program, the compiler reports an error.

- Interfaces help you to structure a piece of code and to make sure that a certain set of functions is implemented.

Algorithms and Data Structures

The syntax of a programming language is only one thing that a programmer has to be familiar with. Algorithms and data structures are at least as important as the syntax of C#. In this chapter, we introduce you to the basic concepts of algorithms and data structures, and show how flexible and extendable software can be written with the help of Mono and C#. You'll learn to perform basic operations and you'll get a feeling for more data-intensive applications as well as performance.

The Mono framework provides a set of classes that help you to do your daily work. In this chapter, we deal with the most basic data structures people need often.

Data Structures

Many of you have dealt with data structures when working with other programming languages. Whenever it's necessary to access information via a standard interface, structures are a good choice. Structures are pretty similar to objects. However, there are also major differences that make it hard to compare structures with objects. Structures are also known as *value types*.

Implementing Structures

Let's see how structures can be implemented. The target of the next example is to implement a data structure that can store a variety of variables:

```
using System;

public struct Product
{
        public string name;
        public double price;
}

public class Demo
{
        public static void Main()
        {
                Product book = new Product();
                book.name = "GNU Mono";
                book.price = 25.49;

                Console.WriteLine("{0}: EUR {1}",
                        book.name, book.price);
        }
}
```

At the beginning of the program, we define a structure called Product that consists of two components. Both components are defined as public, so the variables can be seen inside the main function. The Main method defines a structure and assigns values to it. Afterward, the content of those variables are displayed:

```
[hs@localhost mono]$ mono main.exe
GNU Mono: EUR 25.49
```

Up to now, you haven't seen too many differences between C++ and Mono.

Methods and structures can be combined. The target of the following example is to produce exactly the same output as before:

```
using System;

public struct Product
{
        public string name;
        public double price;

        public void Desc()
        {
```

```
                    Console.WriteLine("{0}: EUR {1}", name, price);
          }
  }

public class Demo
{
          public static void Main()
          {
                    Product book = new Product();
                    book.name = "GNU Mono";
                    book.price = 25.49;

                    book.Desc();
          }
}
```

In this example, we implement a method for displaying information. That way, it's possible to combine the data structure with the logical structure of the program.

The result is the same as before:

```
[hs@localhost mono]$ mono main.exe
GNU Mono: EUR 25.49
```

Structure and Classes

At first glance, classes and structures look pretty similar, but there are some major differences that we want to point out. *Structures* are used to store data and are optimized for that purpose. *Classes* help the programmer to encapsulate data and methods. To achieve that target, features such as inheritance can be used. In contrast to classes, structures act like "sealed classes" rather than other objects. Structures cannot inherit from each other.

System.Collections

The System.Collections namespace contains a set of classes and methods that help the user to work with data structures. All the C programmers among you are familiar with lists and other dynamic data structures. You can easily imagine how much time has been wasted in implementing dynamic data structures in C again and again. Wasting resources because you're repeating the same task too often is not the philosophy that the Mono project reflects. To get rid of inefficient behavior, Mono provides a predefined set of classes that provides all the basic functionalities for managing data.

In this section, we deal with a set of dynamic data structures provided by the Mono framework.

ArrayList

The ArrayList class can be used to store a set of elements. ArrayList provides a *dynamic* data structure, which means that it doesn't store a fixed number of records. The next example shows how data can be retrieved from the user. Let's have a look at some code:

```
using System;
using System.Collections;

public class Demo
{
        public static void Main()
        {
                bool keepdoing = true;
                int  counter = 0;
                string input;
                ArrayList data = new ArrayList();

                // Input
                do
                {
                        Console.WriteLine("Enter some data:");
                        Console.Write("input: ");
                        input = Console.ReadLine();
                        if      (input == "")
                        {
                                keepdoing = false;
                        }
                        else
                        {
                                data.Add(counter);
                                data[counter] = input;
                                counter++;
                        }
                } while (keepdoing == true);

                // display data
                for     (int i = 0; i < counter; i++)
                {
                        Console.WriteLine("Field {0}: {1}", i, data[i]);
```

```
            }
        }
}
```

At the beginning of the example, we define a variable that is able to store an arbitrary amount of data. The user can enter as many records as he wants to. As long as data is entered, the do/while loop is executed. When the user doesn't enter any more data, the loop is terminated and the entire content of the data structure is displayed. Whenever a value is entered into the array, the Add method is called to enlarge the list.

The output might look like this:

```
[hs@localhost mono]$ mono main.exe
Enter some data:
input: dear sir
Enter some data:
input: i am a reader
Enter some data:
input: of this book
Enter some data:
input: and i need help
Enter some data:
input:
Field 0: dear sir
Field 1: i am a reader
Field 2: of this book
Field 3: and i need help
```

The ArrayList object supports a rich set of additional methods. The following list contains an overview of all the important functions:

- BinarySearch: Looks for a special value and returns the index of the element

- Clear: Clears the data structure

- Clone: Copies the data structure

- Contains: Checks whether an element is in the structure.

- IndexOf: Returns the first index of a value

- Insert: Adds an element at a certain position

- LastIndexOf: Returns the last index of a value

- Remove: Removes the first occurrence of an array

- RemoveAt: Removes a special value

- Sort: Sorts an array

BitArray

C/C++ programmers often use bitfields to make data structures more efficient. C# provides methods to optimize code even more. The Mono framework provides an object called BitArray. Various operations with individual bits can be performed with the help of this object.

The following example shows how two bitfields can be combined with the help of And:

```
using System;
using System.Collections;

public class Demo
{
        public static void Main()
        {
                BitArray d1 = new BitArray(3);
                BitArray d2 = new BitArray(3);
                d1[0] = true; d1[1] = false; d1[2] = false;
                d2[0] = true; d2[1] = true; d2[2] = false;

                d1.And(d2);
                Console.WriteLine("0: " + d1[0]);
                Console.WriteLine("1: " + d1[1]);
                Console.WriteLine("2: " + d1[2]);
        }
}
```

Those of you who are familiar with bit operations will not be surprised:

```
[hs@localhost mono]$ mono main.exe
0: True
1: False
2: False
```

The BitArray object provides a set of methods. We've compiled a list of all the important features:

- And: Performs any AND operations

- Clone: Copies an object

- Get: Reads a value in an array

- Not: Inverts all the bit values in the current BitArray

- Or: Performs a bitwise OR operation

- Set: Sets an array

- Xor: Performs a binary XOR

Hashtable

Hashes are a widespread data structure—especially in Perl. Hashes enable the user to access data easily. The Mono framework provides some simple methods for working with hashes. In the next example, you can see how things work:

```
using System;
using System.Collections;

public class Demo
{
        public static void Main()
        {
                Hashtable data = new Hashtable();
                data.Add("Strawberry", 2.2);
                data.Add("Apple", 1.3);
                data.Add("Orange", 1.1);

                Console.WriteLine("Number of elements: " + data.Count);

                Console.WriteLine("Strawberry: " + data["Strawberry"]);
                Console.WriteLine("Apple: " + data["Apple"]);
                Console.WriteLine("Orange: " + data["Orange"]);
        }
}
```

We add many values into the hash and a string is used as the key. This is essential and makes many things simple. In the case of a C program, the situation would be far more complex. To access the data in our data structure, we can use the string you have just seen as an index.

The values are returned correctly:

```
[hs@localhost mono]$ mono main.exe
Number of elements: 3
Strawberry: 2.2
Apple: 1.3
Orange: 1.1
```

`Hashtable` provides the following set of methods:

- `Add`: Adds an element to a hash

- `Clear`: Clears a hash

- `Clone`: Copies a hash

- `Contains`: Checks whether a key can be found inside the hash

- `ContainsKey`: Checks whether a key can be found inside the hash

- `Remove`: Removes values from a hash

Queue

The `System.Collections` namespace contains a class you can use for managing queues. A *queue* is a data structure that contains a set of values. Just like the queue in front of a shop, the data structure is based on the First In, First Out (FIFO) concept. In programming, FIFO means that the record that's added to the data structure first is removed first. This concept is fundamental and many applications are based on it.

The listing shows how you can make use of queues:

```
using System;
using System.Collections;

public class Demo
{
        public static void Main()
        {
                Queue data = new Queue();
                data.Enqueue("contract_2003-09-29.ps");
                data.Enqueue("documentation_postgresql.ps");
                data.Enqueue("help.pdf");

                Console.WriteLine("Number of elements: " + data.Count);

                Console.WriteLine("Element: " + data.Dequeue() );
                Console.WriteLine("Element: " + data.Dequeue() );
                Console.WriteLine("Element: " + data.Dequeue() );
        }
}
```

At the beginning of the application, we define a queue. After that, three elements are added to the data structure. To remove elements from the queue the `Dequeue` method is provided. `Dequeue` returns the first element in the queue and removes it.

In our example, the result will look like this:

```
[hs@localhost mono]$ mono main.exe
Number of elements: 3
Element: contract_2003-09-29.ps
Element: documentation_postgresql.ps
Element: help.pdf
```

The following listing presents the most important methods of `Queue`:

- `Clear`: Deletes a queue

- `Clone`: Copies a queue

- `Contains`: Checks whether the queue contains a certain value

- `Dequeue`: Deletes and returns the first element

- `Enqueue`: Adds a value to the queue

- `Peek`: Returns the first element but does not remove it from the queue

- `TrimToSize`: Defines the maximum size of the queue

SortedList

Accessing sorted data in C/C++ can be painful because it's necessary to implement complex classes to do the job. In case of C#, these classes are already ready for action because they're distributed along with the Mono framework. This saves a lot of work and helps you write consistent applications. With the help of a class named `SortedList`, it's possible to manage sorted lists. This makes sense because sorted lists help to manage data more efficiently.

Let's get started and have a look at an example:

```
using System;
using System.Collections;

public class Demo
{
        public static void Main()
        {
                SortedList data = new SortedList();
                data.Add("Falco", "Rock me Amadeus");
```

```
            data.Add("Juan Luis Guerra", "Burbujas De Amor");
            data.Add("ACDC", "Highway to Hell");

            Console.WriteLine("Size: " + data.Capacity );
            Console.WriteLine("Read only: "
                    + data.IsReadOnly );

            for     (int i = 0; i < data.Count; i++)
            {
                Console.WriteLine("Value {0}: {1}",
                        data.GetKey(i), data.GetByIndex(i) );
            }
        }
}
```

Again we can use Add to add data to the end of the list. Internally, the data is sorted automatically. To see which capacity a list has, Mono provides the right solution for you as well. The Capacity and Count methods inform the user about the size of the data structure. If you want to retrieve information from the sorted list, you can use GetByIndex. To find a key, you can use GetKey.

Let's see what comes out when the program is started:

```
[hs@localhost mono]$ mono main.exe
Size: 16
Read only: False
Value ACDC: Highway to Hell
Value Falco: Rock me Amadeus
Value Juan Luis Guerra: Burbujas De Amor
```

As you might expect, the data is displayed in a sorted order.

Stack

In contrast to queues, stacks are based on the LIFO (Last In, First Out) concept, which means that the last value added to the stack is removed first.

Many algorithms rely on this behavior, and that's why stacks were invented. Two methods are essential when working with stacks: Push adds a value to the stack and Pop removes the most recent value from the stack and returns it.

The next piece of code shows how stacks can be used in C#:

```
using System;
using System.Collections;
```

```
public class Demo
{
        public static void Main()
        {
                Stack data = new Stack();

                data.Push("C/C++");
                data.Push("Perl");
                data.Push("Python");
                data.Push("C#");

                Console.WriteLine("Elements: " + data.Count );
                while   ( data.Count > 0 )
                {
                        Console.WriteLine("Element: {0}", data.Pop() );
                }
        }
}
```

We use Push, Pop, and a variable named Count to implement the program.

The next listing contains the output of the program:

```
[hs@localhost mono]$ mono main.exe
Elements: 4
Element: C#
Element: Python
Element: Perl
Element: C/C++
```

It's important to see that the last value has been removed first.

Collection Interfaces

The Mono framework provides the interfaces that all collections are built on. Whenever it's necessary to implement additional data structures, it's useful to have a look at the proposed standards for data structures. Doing so isn't a must, but it will help you to make your classes fit into the framework.

In the previous section, you saw that all collections work nearly the same way. The reason is that every data structure provided by the Mono framework relies on the same interfaces.

In Brief

- Mono provides a rich set of predefined data structures.

- Structures can help to combine various variables to one object.

- `System.Collections` contains a set of classes for managing data.

- To make programming easy, all classes provide almost the same interface.

- Additional data structures can be implemented easily.

- To implement new data structures, you should stick to collection interfaces.

Managing I/O

C# provides powerful and easy-to-use classes for managing files and directories. The key to the Mono framework and I/O is its simplicity. All classes are high-level interfaces to the underlying operating system. All those among you who are familiar with low-level interfaces to I/O will soon find out that the Mono framework makes your daily life much easier because most of the complexity is hidden by the system.

In this chapter, we deal with the basics of I/O in general. We also see how to use directories, files, and streams.

Working with Directories and Files

The Mono framework provides a variety of classes for managing directories and files. To users familiar with Unix operating systems, this will look strange because there's no reason to deal with directories and files differently. However, in the case of practical work, this difference can make sense.

Let's get started and see which classes we can find in the Mono and, respectively, the .NET frameworks.

- `File`: Contains basic methods for managing files.

- `Directory`: Contains basic methods for managing directories.

- `Path`: Supposed to manage paths. The main idea of this class is to have a mechanism that works fairly independently of the underlying operating system. That's essential because it helps you to write portable code.

- FileInfo: Contains methods for retrieving information about a file.

- DirectoryInfo: Contains methods that you can use to retrieve information about directories.

After that first theoretical overview, it's time to look at some practical examples.

FileInfo

In the following listing, we try to implement a program that displays information about a file:

```
using System;
using System.IO;

public class Demo
{
        public static void Main(string[] args)
        {
                try
                {
                        FileInfo data = new FileInfo(args[0]);

                        Console.WriteLine("Name: " + data.Name);

                        Console.WriteLine("Attributes: "
                                + data.Attributes);
                        Console.WriteLine("Directory: "
                                + data.DirectoryName);
                        Console.WriteLine("ext: " + data.Extension);
                        Console.WriteLine("Length: " + data.Length);
                        Console.WriteLine("Creation time: "
                                + data.CreationTime);
                        Console.WriteLine("Last access: "
                                + data.LastAccessTime);
                        Console.WriteLine("Last modified: "
                                + data.LastWriteTime);
                }
                catch   (Exception e)
                {
                        Console.WriteLine("Error: " + e.Message);
                }
        }
}
```

The first file, which is passed to the program via the command line, is analyzed with the help of the `FileInfo` object. As you can see, all the relevant information is displayed on screen:

```
[hs@localhost mono]$ mono main.exe /etc/passwd
Name: passwd
Attributes: Archive
Directory: /etc
ext:
Length: 1516
Creation time: 03/25/2003 11:39:13
Last access: 04/17/2003 16:05:48
Last modified: 03/25/2003 11:39:13
```

In this example, we used `try` and `catch` to find out whether the file exists. Checks like that can be performed with the help of a member of the instance as well. In the next listing, you can see how that works:

```
using System;
using System.IO;

public class Demo
{
        public static void Main()
        {
                string filename;

                Console.Write("Input: ");
                filename = Console.ReadLine();
                FileInfo data = new FileInfo(filename);
                Console.WriteLine("\nFile exists: " + data.Exists);
        }
}
```

In this case, the name of the file that has to be checked is entered. A member of the instance we created is responsible for telling us whether the file exists:

```
[hs@localhost mono]$ mono main.exe
Input: /etc/passwd

File exists: True
```

The file exists.

The `FileInfo` object provides some more methods that you can use to create or delete a file. In the next example, you learn to create and delete files:

```
using System;
using System.IO;

public class Demo
{
        public static void Main()
        {
                string filename;

                Console.Write("Input: ");
                filename = Console.ReadLine();
                FileInfo data = new FileInfo(filename);

                if      (data.Exists == false)
                {
                        data.Create();
                        Console.WriteLine("The file has been created");
                }
                else
                {
                        data.Delete();
                        Console.WriteLine("The file has been deleted");
                }
        }
}
```

Again, the user has to enter a string containing a filename. If the file does not exist, it's created. If the file is already there, Mono removes it. For creating and removing the file, you can use the methods provided by the `FileInfo` object:

```
[hs@localhost mono]$ mono main.exe
Input: x.cs
The file has been created
[hs@localhost mono]$ mono main.exe
Input: x.cs
The file has been deleted
```

The preceding listing shows what happens when the same name is passed to the program twice.

After those practical examples, it's time for a brief theoretical overview. The next listing provides a summary of the most important operations provided by the `FileInfo` object:

- `AppendText`: Appends text to the file

- `CopyTo`: Copies a file

- `Create`: Creates a file

- `CreateObjRef`: Creates an object reference (useful for remote access)

- `CreateText`: Creates a text file

- `Delete`: Deletes a file

- `Equals`: Compares two instances with each other

- `GetType`: Retrieves the data type of an instance

- `MoveTo`: Moves a file

- `Open`: Opens a file

- `OpenRead`: Opens a file for reading

- `OpenText`: Opens a file for operations related to text

- `Refresh`: Retrieves the status of an object again

DirectoryInfo

The `DirectoryInfo` object can be used to manage directories. In the next example, you learn to retrieve information about directories. Keep in mind that the actual output of the program depends on the operating system you're using:

```
using System;
using System.IO;

public class Demo
{
        public static void Main(string[] args)
        {
                if      (args.Length > 0)
                {
                        DirectoryInfo data = new DirectoryInfo(args[0]);
                        Console.WriteLine("Name: "
                                + data.FullName);
                        Console.WriteLine("Attributes: "
                                + data.Attributes);
                        Console.WriteLine("Parent: " + data.Parent);
                        Console.WriteLine("Root: " + data.Root);
```

```
                    Console.WriteLine("Creation time: "
                            + data.CreationTime);
                    Console.WriteLine("Last access: "
                            + data.LastAccessTime);
                    Console.WriteLine("Last modified: "
                            + data.LastWriteTime);

                }

        }

}
```

We read the name of the directory, the attributes, the parent node, and the root node as well as various timestamps. Most values provided by the object are similar to the ones provided by `FileInfo`. However, there are some major differences that occur when running the program:

```
[hs@localhost mono]$ mono main.exe /usr/local/src/
Name: /usr/local/src/
Attributes: Directory
Parent: src
Root:
Creation time: 02/06/1996 22:04:01
Last access: 04/17/2003 15:07:40
Last modified: 02/06/1996 22:04:01
```

In this scenario, the name of the parent node is similar to the name of the child node. The reason for that is because we added a slash to the end of the path. If the slash at the end of the path is removed, the result differs significantly:

```
[hs@localhost mono]$ mono main.exe /usr/local/src
Name: /usr/local/src
Attributes: Directory
Parent: local
Root:
Creation time: 02/06/1996 22:04:01
Last access: 04/17/2003 15:07:40
Last modified: 02/06/1996 22:04:01
```

As you can easily imagine, this is a source of troubles because when looking at the world from a Unix point of view, the two paths are almost identical and have the same meaning.

More recent versions of Mono return `local`. There is no problem with slashes anymore. This has been fixed for Mono because it has been fixed for .NET 1.1 as well.

It's important to mention that Microsoft's implementation of this function works the same way, so you must be aware of this fact.

The following list presents the most important methods provided by the `DirectoryInfo` class:

- `Create`: Creates a directory

- `CreateObjRef`: Creates a reference to the object

- `CreateSubdirectory`: Creates a subdirectory

- `Delete`: Deletes a directory

- `Equals`: Checks whether two instances are the same

- `GetDirectories`: Returns a list of all directories in a certain directory

- `GetFiles`: Returns a list of all files in a certain directory

- `GetType`: Returns the data type of a variable

- `MoveTo`: Moves a directory

- `Refresh`: Refreshes the status of the object

To make the methods you just saw a little bit clearer, we've compiled an example. In the following listing, you can see how a list of all directories can be generated:

```
using System;
using System.IO;

public class Demo
{
        public static void Main(string[] args)
        {
                foreach (string x in args)
                {
                        Console.WriteLine("directories in {0}", x);
                        DirectoryInfo dir = new DirectoryInfo(x);
                        DirectoryInfo[] myinfo = dir.GetDirectories();
                        foreach (DirectoryInfo s in myinfo)
                        {
                                Console.WriteLine(s);
                        }

                        Console.WriteLine("\nfiles in {0}", x);
                        FileInfo[] files = dir.GetFiles();
                        foreach (FileInfo s in files)
                        {
                                Console.WriteLine(s);
```

```
                    }

              }

         }

    }
```

We process all directories passed to the program via standard input. This is done with the help of an ordinary loop. As long as a valid string can be found, we try to list all subdirectories and files in the directory. The list returned by the object is processed using foreach loops. The algorithm is used to list the desired files.

```
[hs@localhost mono]$ mono main.exe /usr/local/pgsql/include/
directories in /usr/local/pgsql/include/
internal
libpq

files in /usr/local/pgsql/include/
/usr/local/pgsql/include/ecpgerrno.h
/usr/local/pgsql/include/ecpglib.h
/usr/local/pgsql/include/ecpgtype.h
/usr/local/pgsql/include/libpgeasy.h
/usr/local/pgsql/include/libpq-fe.h
/usr/local/pgsql/include/pg_config.h
/usr/local/pgsql/include/pg_config_os.h
/usr/local/pgsql/include/postgres_ext.h
/usr/local/pgsql/include/sql3types.h
/usr/local/pgsql/include/sqlca.h
```

Mono displays the full path to the files. Microsoft's .NET does not provide the full path here. This is a difference that has to be taken into consideration when dealing with Mono and when writing portable applications.

This behavior should be considered a bug in Mono. It will be fixed in future versions so as to behave as close to the Microsoft manner as possible.

Streams

Streams are a fundamental concept. In general, streams are nothing more than a sequence of data. The way streams work in C# is pretty similar to Java. Most I/O functions provided by the Mono framework are based on streams, which shows how important dealing with streams is.

Mono provides a set of efficient classes for working with streams. One thing that these classes have in common is that they've all been derived from a parent class called Stream.

Let's see the classes we're talking about (Stream and read/write classes):

- BinaryReader: Reads basic data types

- BinaryWriter: Writes basic data types

- BufferedStream: Provides mechanisms to deal with buffered streams

- CryptoStream: Provides interfaces to algorithms for encrypting data

- FileStream: Enables the user to access files

- MemoryStream: Enables the user to manage data in memory

- NetworkStream: Provides interfaces to networking protocols

- StreamReader: Reads characters from a stream

- StreamWriter: Writes characters into a stream

- StringReader: Reads strings

- StringWriter: Writes strings

In the next section, we focus on the most basic operations that you can perform with the help of streams.

Reading and Writing Data

Reading and writing files is undoubtedly important. With the help of C#, those two tasks are quite simple. In the next example, we focus on simple I/O operations:

```
using System;
using System.IO;

public class Demo
{
        public static int Main()
        {
                string file = "/etc/passwd";
                int lines = 5;
                string tmp;

                try
                {
                        // Opens a file stream
                        FileStream input = new FileStream(
                                file,
```

```
                        System.IO.FileMode.Open,
                        System.IO.FileAccess.Read);
            StreamReader reading = new StreamReader(input);

            // read the first line
            for     (int i = 0; i < 5; i++)
            {
                    tmp = reading.ReadLine();
                    Console.WriteLine("{0}: {1}", i, tmp);
            }

            // closes the streams
            reading.Close();
        }
        catch   (Exception e)
        {
            Console.WriteLine("Error: " + e.Message);
            return 1;
        }

        return 0;
    }
}
```

In this example, we read the first five lines of /etc/passwd and create a stream called input. This stream is used to read data from the file. As soon as we open the stream, we can create an instance of StreamReader. We need this instance to retrieve data from the file. In our example, we need exactly five lines. Reading one line can be done with the help of the ReadLine method. Now we can go ahead and display the data on screen. After processing the loop, we close the instance of the object we used to read the data.

The output of the program could look like this:

```
[hs@localhost mono]$ mono main.exe
0: root:x:0:0:root:/root:/bin/bash
1: bin:x:1:1:bin:/bin:/sbin/nologin
2: daemon:x:2:2:daemon:/sbin:/sbin/nologin
3: adm:x:3:4:adm:/var/adm:/sbin/nologin
4: lp:x:4:7:lp:/var/spool/lpd:/sbin/nologin
```

Now that you've seen how to read data from a file, you can see how data could be written into a file:

```
using System;
using System.IO;

public class Demo
{
        public static int Main(string[] args)
        {
                string file = "/tmp/mono.txt";

                try
                {
                        FileStream outix = new FileStream(file,
                                        System.IO.FileMode.OpenOrCreate,
                                        System.IO.FileAccess.Write);
                        StreamWriter writing = new StreamWriter(outix);

                        for     (int i = 0; i < args.Length; i++)
                        {
                                writing.WriteLine(args[i]);
                        }

                        writing.Close();
                        outix.Close();
                }
                catch   (Exception e)
                {
                        Console.WriteLine("Error: " + e.Message);
                        return 1;
                }

                return 0;
        }
}
```

An instance of FileStream is created at the beginning of the file. In this case, we want to write data into the file. We tell Mono that the file we want to send the data to should be opened or created. To write the data, an instance of StreamWriter is generated. In our example, the data passed to the program via the command-line interface has to be sent to the stream. To perform the write operation, the WriteLine method is needed.

The output might look like this:

```
[hs@duron io]$ mono file.exe hello world
[hs@duron io]$ cat /tmp/mono.txt
hello
world
```

On some versions of Mono, this example does not compile.

Both words are added to the end of the file. It's important to examine the end of the line. In this example, Mono uses a linefeed. That's important because in this situation Mono is different from Windows. Future versions of Mono will use the Windows line endings when running Mono on Windows platforms.

After that example, let's look at the most basic methods provided by the `FileStream` class:

- `BeginRead`: Starts to read asynchronously

- `BeginWrite`: Begins an asynchronous writing operation

- `Close`: Closes the stream

- `EndRead`: Ends the operation

- `EndWrite`: Stops asynchronous writing

- `Equals`: Checks whether two pieces of data are the same

- `Flush`: Flushes the buffer

- `Lock`: Locks the file so that other users cannot access it

- `Read`: Reads data and writes it into a buffer

- `ReadByte`: Reads one byte and moves the file pointer to the next file

- `Seek`: Goes to the desired position

- `SetLength`: Sets the length of the stream

- `Unlock`: Removes a lock

- `Write`: Writes data into the buffer

- `WriteByte`: Writes one byte

In addition, the class provides several properties. The next list describes the most important ones:

- `CanRead`: Tells the user whether a string can be read

- `CanSeek`: Tells the user whether it's allowed to change the position inside the stream

- `CanWrite`: Tells the user whether it's allowed to write data into the stream

- `Handle`: Contains the file handle of the underlying operating system

- `IsAsync`: Tells us whether a stream is synchronous or asynchronous

- `Length`: Contains the length of the stream

- `Name`: Tells the name of the stream we passed to the constructor

- `Position`: Tells the user the current position inside the stream

In Mono, it's possible to define the mode in which the stream should be accessed. In our examples, we used `System.IO.FileMode.OpenOrCreate` and `System.IO.FileMode.Open`. The following list contains an overview of the most important settings:

- `Append`: Adds data to a stream

- `Create`: Creates a file or adds data to a file

- `CreateNew`: Creates a new file or displays an error

- `Open`: Opens a file

- `OpenOrCreate`: Opens an existing file or creates a new file

- `Truncate`: Opens a file and deletes the content

- `Read`: Opens a file for reading it

- `ReadWrite`: Opens a file for reading and writing

- `Write`: Writes into a file

Encoding

After this basic introduction to streams, we must deal with an additional topic that's extremely important. Streams can have many different encodings. Up to now, we've assumed that data is always ASCII encoded. However, ASCII is not always enough and Mono provides much more flexibility and offers a number of encodings. In the case of .NET, all strings are Unicode (Unicode Transformation Format-16le) encoded. This makes sense because every character can be displayed. Keep in mind that a character needs more than one byte of storage—this is an important subject that you must take into consideration.

In the next example, we see how line numbers can be added to a file and how the content can be transformed to UTF-8–encoded (UTF-8) data. With the help of UTF-8 code, it's possible to store many more different characters than with the help of an 8-bit character set:

```csharp
using System;
using System.IO;
using System.Text;

public class Demo
{
        public static int Main(string[] args)
        {
                StreamReader read;
                read = new StreamReader(File.OpenRead("input.txt"),
                        Encoding.ASCII);

                StreamWriter write;
                write = new StreamWriter(File.OpenWrite("output.txt"),
                        Encoding.UTF8);

                int line = 0;
                while (true)
                {
                        string str = read.ReadLine();
                        if (str == null) break;
                        line++;
                        write.WriteLine("{0:D4} {1}", line, str);
                }
                read.Close();
                write.Close();

                return 0;
        }
}
```

At the beginning of the file, we create an instance of the `StreamReader` object and we open a file. Therefore, we use the `File` object and a method called Open. To manage the output, we create an instance of the `StreamWriter` object. We make sure that the output is UTF-8 encoded. Finally, we process the input stream line by line and increment `line` every time the loop is executed. We use this information as the line number. To make sure that four digits are used, the output format is defined when calling the `WriteLine` method. After processing the file, we close all streams.

The input file could look like this:

```
This is a text
we will use to
```

work with Mono
and I/O in general.
I hope it works.

That input leads to the following output:

```
0001 This is a text
0002 we will use to
0003 work with Mono
0004 and I/O in general.
0005 I hope it works.
0006
```

Future versions of Mono will add UTF-8 byte order marks to the beginning of the text.

Working with Binary Files

Whenever data has to be stored more efficiently, or whenever it's necessary to hide data from the user, a binary file format is a good choice. C# provides methods for working with binary files. In the next example, we deal with binary numbers and see how binary information can be stored in a file:

```csharp
using System;
using System.IO;

public class Demo
{
        public static int Main(string[] args)
        {
                string filename = "/tmp/file.bin";
                int data;
                int x = args.Length;
                int i;

                // Writes values
                BinaryWriter bw = new BinaryWriter(
                        File.Create(filename));

                for     ( i = 0; i < x; i++ )
                {
                        try
                        {
                                data = Int32.Parse(args[i]);
                                bw.Write( data );
```

```
                    Console.WriteLine("Writing: " + data);
            }
            catch (Exception e)
            {
                    Console.WriteLine("Input error");
            }
        }

    bw.Close();

    // Reading binary values
    BinaryReader br = new BinaryReader(
            File.OpenRead(filename));
    int ausgabe;

    while    (true)
    {
            try
            {
                    ausgabe = br.ReadInt32();
                    Console.WriteLine("Output: "
                            + ausgabe);
            }
            catch (Exception e)
            {
                    break;
            }
        }
        br.Close();

        return 0;
    }
}
```

The target of the program is to store all data passed to the script via standard input in binary format. To store data in a file, we create an instance of `BinaryWriter`. This instance is responsible for writing the binary data stream. We process every value and try to convert every string to an integer value. Therefore, the `Parse` method has to be called for the `Int32` object. As long as no error occurs, the values are added to the file.

To display the data we stored in the file, we open a `BinaryStream`. The various values in the file are read by the `ReadInt32` method. If the end of the stream is reached, the loop is terminated by the `break` command.

Let's see what happens when we execute the program:

```
[hs@localhost mono]$ mono main.exe 1 2 3 error 6
Writing: 1
Writing: 2
Writing: 3
Input error
Writing: 6
Output: 1
Output: 2
Output: 3
Output: 6
```

The data is written and read correctly.

When working with binary streams, two classes are fundamental. The `BinaryReader` class provides the following methods:

- `Close`: Closes the stream

- `PeekChar`: Returns the next character but does not modify the file pointer

- `Read`: Reads data from the stream and moves the file pointer to the next position

- `ReadBoolean`: Reads a Boolean value

- `ReadByte`: Reads one byte

- `ReadBytes`: Reads various bytes

- `ReadChar`: Reads one character

- `ReadChars`: Reads multiple characters

- `ReadDecimal`: Reads a decimal value

- `ReadDouble`: Reads a double value

- `ReadInt16`: Reads a 2-byte integer value

- `ReadInt32`: Reads a 4-byte integer value

- `ReadInt64`: Reads an 8-byte integer value

- `ReadSByte`: Reads a signed byte

- `ReadSingle`: Reads a 4-byte float

- `ReadUInt16`: Reads an unsigned 2-byte integer value

- `ReadUInt32`: Reads an unsigned 4-byte integer value

- `ReadUInt64`: Reads an unsigned 8-byte integer value

The `BinaryWriter` class is also essential. The following list describes the available methods:

- `Close`: Closes the stream

- `Flush`: Flushes the buffer to disk

- `Seek`: Moves to the desired position inside the stream

- `Write`: Write data into the stream

Managing Data in Memory

Sometimes it's far too slow to store data on a hard drive. To increase the performance of an application, you can store data in memory. Therefore, C# provides mechanisms to help you to manage memory.

In general, `MemoryStream` works just like the `FileStream` class, so we won't deal with this class in detail because it's far beyond the scope of this book.

Object Serialization

When talking about I/O in general, its important to think of object serialization. Before we see how objects can be serialized, it's necessary to understand the fundamental concepts of this topic. Assume that a complex object provides a rich set of attributes. When writing the object to disk, it's necessary to find a suitable format in which to store the data efficiently. More than that, it can be necessary to have easy-to-use interfaces that make it possible to quickly implement software. Luckily, C# and the Mono framework provide such interfaces.

Mono's onboard tools for object serialization take an instance and transform it to a string. This string be can saved to disk. Of course, reading data from disk and making an instance out of it works as well. Especially in the case of complex applications, having a standard interface for making strings of objects is essential because it saves a lot of work.

In this section, we look at object serialization in general and examine some basic examples.

Serialization and XML

In many cases, XML is a good choice for working with serialized objects. XML has many advantages because every data source can be easily modeled with XML. In addition, XML is a standard for describing data. Mono and XML are closely related. XML is a fundamental component of Mono. .NET provides a rich set of interfaces for XML, so Mono is supposed to support XML as well. For serializing objects, several classes are essential. All the important objects can be found in the `System.Xml.Serialization` namespace. In general, serializing data works like this:

```
MyClass obj = new MyClass(...)
TextWriter txt = new StreamWriter("dataafile.xml");
XmlSerializer serial = new XmlSerializer(typeof(MyClass));
Serial.Serialize(txt, obj);
txt.Close();
```

We define an instance of the XmlSerializer object. After that, we define the stream to which the result should be sent. Because C# provides a lot of flexibility, you can decide which kind of stream should be used. Particularly when information should be sent across networks, this is essential.

To load serialized data, you can use the following algorithm:

```
FileStream fs_read = new FileStream("datafile.xml", FileMode.Open);
XmlSerializer serial_read = new XmlSerializer(typeof(MyClass));
MyClass read_obj = (MyClass) serial_read.Deserialize(fs_read);
fs_read.Close();
```

Again, we need just a few lines to solve the problem.

Proprietary Serialization

In some cases, the standard methods for serializing objects might not be what you're looking for. Whenever it's necessary to use certain file formats or optimize the way data is stored, proprietary solutions are a good approach.

We don't cover proprietary implementations because they're far beyond the scope of this book.

In Brief

- Mono provides classes for managing files and directories.

- Mono defines a difference between files and directory so that different classes have to be used.

- I/O is based on streams.

- Depending on the type of I/O, different kinds of streams must be used.

- Binary files can help make your storage system more efficient.

- Classes must be serialized before writing them to disk

Strings and Regular Expressions

Strings are basic elements that you'll need in almost every kind of application. Because of the importance of strings, the Mono framework provides many classes and features for managing strings fast and efficiently.

Regular expressions are the perfect tool for finding patterns and special sequences of characters. Whenever it's necessary to look for something that isn't defined properly but is fuzzy, regular expressions might provide the right solution.

In this chapter, it's time to have a look at strings and regular expressions.

Working with Strings

Let's get started and see how you can work with strings. We recommend going through this section carefully so that you can use this information in the chapters that are still to come.

Working with strings is so important that we decided to present an example for every method related to your daily work with strings. Understanding these examples is essential for understanding the rest of the book.

Comparing Strings

To compare two strings with each other, C# provides two methods. The Compare method is a static method that accepts two values. In contrast to Compare, the CompareTo method is called for an instance. This is a major difference, although the output of those two methods is the same.

Let's look at an example and see how strings can be compared:

```
using System;

public class Demo
{
        public static void Main()
        {
                string a = "Arno Arens";
                string b = "Zagory Meyers";

                // comparing strings
                Console.WriteLine("simple: "
                        + String.Compare(a, b));
                Console.WriteLine("simple: "
                        + String.Compare(b, a));

                // working with offset
                Console.WriteLine("\nusing offset: "
                        + String.Compare(a, 1, b, 1, 3));
                Console.WriteLine("using offset: "
                        + String.Compare(b, 1, a, 1, 3));

                // case insensitive
                Console.WriteLine("\nCase insensitive: "
                        + String.Compare(b, 1, a, 1, 3, true));

                Console.WriteLine("\nUsing an instance: "
                        + a.CompareTo(b));
        }
}
```

When you call Compare, two strings are compared. Depending on the two strings you're passing to the function, the result will differ. If both strings are the same, 0 will be returned.

The Compare method is overloaded. Some of these overloadings have already been presented in previous examples. If four parameters are passed to the function, an offset is used. The fourth parameter defines which characters should be compared with each other. The fifth parameter tells the system whether the search is case sensitive or case insensitive.

Let's see which result is generated by the system:

```
[hs@localhost mono]$ mono main.exe
simple: -1
simple: 1
```

```
using offset: 1
using offset: -1

Case insensitive: -1

Using an instance: -1
```

An additional method you can utilize to compare strings is `Equals`. The following listing shows how the method works:

```csharp
using System;

public class Demo
{
        public static void Main()
        {
                string a, b, c;

                a = "Hugo";
                b = "Peter";

                Console.WriteLine( String.Equals(a, b) );
                Console.WriteLine( a == b );
        }
}
```

The return value of a comparison can be either `True` or `False`, depending on whether the two strings are the same. In this example, the strings we compared are different, so the result is `False`:

```
[hs@duron regexp]$ mono file.exe
False
False
```

As you saw in the listing, the `==` operator is the same as the `Equals` function.

Connecting Strings

Combining multiple strings into one big string can be done with the help of methods as well. In the case of Mono and C#, you can make use of `Concat`, which works as follows:

```csharp
using System;

public class Demo
{
```

```
public static void Main()
{
        string a = "Joe Clay ";
        string b = "is in love";

        Console.WriteLine("News: " +
                String.Concat(a, b));
    }
}
```

We pass two parameters to the method. The result of the operation is returned as a string. In the next listing, you can see what the program displays on screen:

```
[hs@localhost mono]$ mono main.exe
News: Joe Clay is in love
```

The Concat method can do much more than just connecting two strings with each other. Mono provides a set of overloadings that will help you concatenate many kinds of objects:

- Concat(Object[])

- Concat(String[])

- Concat(Object, Object)

- Concat(Object, Object, Object)

- Concat(string, string, string)

- Concat(string, string, string, string)

An additional method for concatenating strings is the Join method. Especially when it's necessary to make use of arrays, Join is far more comfortable to use than Concat.

In this listing, we deal with Join in detail:

```
using System;

public class Demo
{
        public static void Main()
        {
                string[] a = new string[] {
                        "Alfred Altenhofer",
                        "Zagory Meyers",
                        "Heino Markas" };
```

```
          Console.WriteLine( string.Join(", ", a) );
      }
}
```

We pass two parameters to the method. The first parameter contains a string that is used as a separator between the strings and the array. The second parameter contains an array containing the strings we want to connect:

```
[hs@localhost mono]$ mono main.exe
Alfred Altenhofer, Zagory Meyers, Heino Markas
```

If you don't like to use methods to concatenate strings, you can make use of the + operator instead.

Copying Strings

Copying strings is an important task, and not just in C#. In this section, you learn how copying strings works with C#:

```
using System;

public class Demo
{
      public static void Main()
      {
            string a, b, c;

            a = "Peter";
            b = String.Copy(a);

            c = a;
            a = "Hugo";

            Console.WriteLine("a: {0}, b: {1}, c: {2}", a, b, c);
      }
}
```

First, we define three variables and we assign a value to the first variable. This value is copied and the result is assigned to b. After we assign a to c, we assign a string to a. Finally the output is displayed:

```
[hs@localhost mono]$ mono main.exe
a: Hugo, b: Peter, c: Peter
```

It's important to mention that c does not have the value of a. To copy the content of a variable, you can call the `Clone` method. Most objects know this method, so it's fairly easy to clone objects. The next example shows how things work:

```
using System;

public class Demo
{
        public static void Main()
        {
                string a = "www.postgresql.at";
                string b = (string) a.Clone();
                Console.WriteLine( b );
        }
}
```

When copying a string, it's important to cast the result to `string`. This is essential because otherwise the compiler will report an error.

The output of the program can be found in the following listing:

```
[hs@localhost mono]$ mono main.exe
www.postgresql.at
```

Displaying Strings

In most applications, strings have to be displayed in a certain format. Therefore the Mono framework provides easy-to-use methods that make daily life with the language much easier:

```
using System;

public class Demo
{
        public static void Main()
        {
                string a = "Hello World";
                Console.WriteLine( "Length: " + a.Length );
                Console.WriteLine( "Left: " + a.PadLeft(20) );
                Console.WriteLine( "Right: " + a.PadRight(20) );
        }
}
```

`PadRight` and `PadLeft` help you display a string of a certain length by adding space characters to the left or to the right side of the string. Just pass the desired length of the string to the method, and C# does the rest for you.

Let's see which result we can expect from the example you just saw:

```
[hs@localhost mono]$ mono main.exe
Length: 11
Left:          Hello World
Right: Hello World
```

It's sometimes necessary to analyze the string to find out where a certain element can be found. In the case of C#, you can use the IndexOf method to do the job:

```
using System;

public class Demo
{
        public static void Main()
        {
                string a = "Hello World";
                Console.WriteLine("Position: " + a.IndexOf('l') );
        }
}
```

We're trying to find the position of the first l inside the string. Therefore, the desired symbol has to be passed to the IndexOf method. The position of the substring is returned:

```
[hs@localhost mono]$ mono main.exe
Position: 2
```

Don't forget that you must use double quotation marks when passing the character to the method; otherwise, an error will be reported.

Like most methods in the Mono framework, IndexOf has been overloaded:

- IndexOf(char);

- IndexOf(string);

- IndexOf(char, beginInt);

- IndexOf(char, beginInt);

- IndexOf(string, beginInt);

- IndexOf(char, beginInt, endInt);

- IndexOf(char, beginInt, endInt);

- IndexOf(string, beginInt, endInt);

IndexOf looks for the first position in which a character can be found. If you're looking for the last time something can be found in a string, you need to use the LastIndexOf method.

In many cases, strings start or end with whitespace characters. Whitespace characters are characters that look like blanks when they're displayed on the screen. In reality, a blank is not the only symbol that looks like a blank. It's always better to look for whitespace characters than for blanks to make sure that no character is omitted accidentally.

In the next example, you learn how whitespace characters can be removed:

```
using System;

public class Demo
{
        public static void Main()
        {
                string a = "  Hello World  ";
                Console.WriteLine("length before: " + a.Length );

                string b = a.Trim();
                Console.WriteLine("after Trim: " + b );
                Console.WriteLine("length after Trim: "
                        + b.Length );

                string c = a.TrimEnd();
                Console.WriteLine("after TrimEnd: " + c );
                Console.WriteLine("length after TrimEnd: "
                        + c.Length );
        }
}
```

Trim is a method that you can use to cut off whitespace characters. Note that Trim cuts off characters at the beginning and end of a string. In contrast, TrimStart takes care of only the beginning of a string. TrimEnd is the counterpart of TrimStart and can be used to cut off whitespace characters at the end of a string.

In the next listing, you can see what comes out when the program is started:

```
[hs@localhost mono]$ mono main.exe
length before: 15
after Trim: Hello World
length after Trim: 11
after TrimEnd:   Hello World
length after TrimEnd: 13
```

Finally, it's time to take a closer look at case-sensitive operations:

```
using System;

public class Demo
{
        public static void Main()
        {
                string a = "Austrians are no Germans for sure";
                Console.WriteLine( a.ToUpper() );
                Console.WriteLine( a.ToLower() );
        }
}
```

In general, two methods are essential. The ToUpper function converts a string to uppercase letters. In contrast, the ToLower function makes sure that a string is returned in lowercase letters.

Let's see how an important fact is treated by C#:

```
[hs@localhost mono]$ mono main.exe
AUSTRIANS ARE NO GERMANS FOR SURE
austrians are no germans for sure
```

Modifying Strings—Adding and Removing Characters

Whenever it's necessary to add characters to a string or when characters have to be removed from a string, Insert and Remove are essential. Let's take a look at those two methods:

```
using System;

public class Demo
{
        public static void Main()
        {
                string a = "Hello World";
                a = a.Remove(6, 5);
                Console.WriteLine("before: " + a );

                a = a.Insert(6, "Reader");
                Console.WriteLine("after: " + a );

        }
}
```

Five characters are removed from the string. After that, some characters are added to the string. The result of this operation is shown in the next listing:

```
[hs@localhost mono]$ mono main.exe
before: Hello
after: Hello Reader
```

A copy of the string is returned by these operations. If it wasn't reassigned, it would still hold the "before" text.

Converting Strings

When implementing complex applications, it can be necessary to change the data type of a variable. This is normally a crucial operation that can lead to severe problems. At first sight, many newbies will miss functions such as atoi (ASCII to integer). Most conversions can be done with the help of static methods. If you want to convert a string to integer, you can use a method of the Int64 class.

Let's examine the next example and see how the problem can be solved:

```
using System;

public class Demo
{
        public static void Main(string[] args)
        {
                long input;

                try
                {
                        input = Int64.Parse(args[0]);
                        Console.WriteLine("number: " + input);
                }
                catch (Exception e)
                {
                        Console.WriteLine("error ... " );
                }
        }
}
```

The first parameter that's passed to the program is converted to Int64. To perform the cast, we use the Parse method.

After reading the number, it is displayed on screen. If casting the string doesn't work, an error is reported. In the following example, you can see the result you can expect:

```
[hs@localhost mono]$ mono main.exe 4323
number: 4323
```

You have just seen that strings can be converted to other data types. However, it's also possible to convert a string to an array of bytes. In the next example, we look at byte arrays:

```
using System;

public class Demo
{
        public static void Main()
        {
                string a = "Hello reader";
                byte[] mybytes = System.Text.Encoding.ASCII.GetBytes(a);

                foreach (byte i in mybytes)
                {
                        Console.WriteLine("{0} - {1}",
                                Convert.ToChar(i), i);
                }
        }
}
```

At the beginning of the code, we define a string. This string is converted. We use GetBytes to do the job. After calling the method, we can display one value after the other.

In addition to the character itself, we display the ASCII value of the symbol:

```
[hs@localhost mono]$ mono main.exe
H - 72
e - 101
l - 108
l - 108
o - 111
  - 32
r - 114
e - 101
a - 97
d - 100
e - 101
r - 114
```

If you don't want to use an array to store bytes, you can use the char data type. The next example uses arrays so that you see how we can pick a certain character in the array:

```
using System;

public class Demo
{
        public static void Main()
        {
                string a = "PostgreSQL, SAP DB, DB2";
                char[] myarray = a.ToCharArray();

                Console.WriteLine( myarray[0] );
        }
}
```

The output of the program is not surprising:

```
[hs@localhost mono]$ mono main.exe
P
```

The same result could have been achieved differently:

```
Console.WriteLine( a[0] );
```

Splitting Strings

If you want to split a string in order to make an array of substrings out of it, you can utilize a method called Split, which is part of the Mono framework. C#'s Split method is similar to Perl's mechanism for splitting strings. All you have to do is to define a symbol that is needed to split the string. C# returns an array that contains the substrings.

The following code is an example of using Split:

```
using System;

public class Demo
{
        public static void Main()
        {
                string a = "PostgreSQL,SAP DB,DB2";
                string[] myarray = a.Split(new char[] {','} );

                foreach (string str in myarray)
```

```
                {
                        Console.WriteLine( str );
                }
        }
}
```

As you can see, the string is split into three strings that are displayed in the next listing:

```
[hs@localhost mono]$ mono main.exe
PostgreSQL
SAP DB
DB2
```

Substrings

Whenever it's necessary to extract a substring, you should consider the Substring method. Two parameters have to be passed to the method. The first parameter defines the starting position inside the string. The second parameter tells Mono how many characters should be read.

To demonstrate the behavior of Substring, we've compiled an example:

```
using System;

public class Demo
{
        public static void Main()
        {
                string a = "PostgreSQL, SAP DB, DB2";
                Console.WriteLine( "I love " + a.Substring(0, 10) );
        }
}
```

We extract the word PostgreSQL and display the text on the screen:

```
[hs@localhost mono]$ mono main.exe
I love PostgreSQL
```

StringBuilder

The StringBuilder class can be used to modify and compile strings. It provides fundamental operations, such as appending characters and removing characters from a string. When modifying strings, we recommend using StringBuilder instead of ordinary strings because StringBuilder can help you to raise the performance of your application.

In the next example, we look at some fundamental operations:

```
using System;
using System.Text;

public class Demo
{
        public static void Main()
        {
                // Combining strings
                string dazu = "with C#";
                StringBuilder str = new StringBuilder("See Sharp ");
                str.Append( dazu );
                Console.WriteLine( str );

                // Ensuring capacities
                str.EnsureCapacity( str.Length + 100 );

                // Adding data
                str.AppendFormat( "{0,2}", " and Mono");
                Console.WriteLine( str );

                // Adding characters
                str.Insert(0, "News: ");
                Console.WriteLine( str );

                // Displaying information
                Console.WriteLine("Length: " + str.Length);
                Console.WriteLine("Cap.: " + str.MaxCapacity);
        }
}
```

At the beginning of the program, a string is defined. With the help of StringBuilder, we add some characters to the string. The result is displayed and we make sure that the instance of StringBuilder has a guaranteed capacity.

To add a formatted string, you can use AppendFormat. To add characters to the string, Insert is the method that should be employed.

At the end of the program, we display the length and the maximum capacity (in recent version of Mono, a string can hold 2^{31} characters) of the string we generated. Let's see what comes out when we start the program:

```
[hs@localhost mono]$ mono main.exe
See Sharp with C#
```

```
See Sharp with C# and Mono
News: See Sharp with C# and Mono
Length: 32
Cap.: 2147483647
```

Regular Expressions

Regular expressions are a performance boost for your application. In addition, regular expressions will help you to efficiently solve complex problems. This will save you a lot of headache and a lot of code. Problems that are nearly impossible to solve can be treated easily.

Although we've used regular expressions for years, there are still new features to be discovered. There is a lot of potential that can help you to achieve your targets.

This chapter isn't supposed to be an introduction to regular expressions. It's just an overview of what can be done with the help of C# and Mono. You'll also see what you have to take into consideration when you use regular expressions.

Overview

In this section, you'll see how regular expressions work and which special characters are supported by C#. We assume that every reader has some basic experience with regular expressions.

The following listing contains an overview of all the important symbols:

- `.`: Matches every symbol but linefeeds.

- `[abc]`: Matches every character in the list.

- `[A-Za-z0-9]`: Matches every letter and every number.

- `[^abc]`: Matches every letter but the ones in the list.

- `\w`: Matches a word.

- `\W`: Matches characters that cannot appear in a word.

- `\s`: Matches a whitespace character such as (`\n\f\t\r`).

- `\S`: Matches a nonwhitespace character.

- `\d`: Matches numbers.

- `\D`: Matches symbols that are not numbers (this is equal to `[^0-9]`.

- `^`: Matches the beginning of a line.

- $: Matches the end of a line.

- \b: Matches the borders of a word.

- \B: Matches every character that does not symbolize the border of a word.

- *: At least zero matches.

- +: At least one match.

- ?: Zero or one match.

- {*n*}: Exactly *n* matches.

- {*n*,}: At least *n* matches.

- {n,m}: At least *n* but not more than *m* matches.

- (): Marks a group. With the help of brackets, you can create groups inside the regular expression.

- (?<*name*>): Marks an expression and assigns it to a name.

- ¦: Marks an OR.

If special characters are not used as special characters, it's necessary to escape them. *Escaping* means that a special character is not treated as such. A character can be escaped by using a backslash. Let's look at an example:

```
\{abc\}
```

The expression you see in the listing means that the string abc is found when it is inside parentheses.

Searching

In the next example, you'll learn to use regular expressions in combination with a string:

```
using System;
using System.Text.RegularExpressions;

public class Demo
{
        public static void Main()
        {
                string pattern = "Hello reader";

                Regex reg = new Regex("^Hello");
```

```
            Match mat = reg.Match( pattern );
            Console.WriteLine("found: " + mat);
        }
}
```

At the beginning of the program, we define a string. To create a regular expression, the constructor of the Regex has to be called. After that, an instance of the Match object is defined. We need this instance because it's supposed to store the match found by the regular expression. Finally, the string is displayed:

```
[hs@localhost mono]$ mono main.exe
found: Hello
```

In our case, we want to know whether a substring has been found. Therefore, the method called Success can be called. To find out whether True is returned, you can use an If statement. The next piece of code includes two examples:

```
using System;
using System.Text.RegularExpressions;

public class Demo
{
        public static void Main()
        {
                string pattern = "Hello Reader";
                Regex reg = new Regex("^Hello");
                Match mat = reg.Match( pattern );

                // alternatively:
                // if    (mat.Success)
                if      (mat.Success == true)
                {
                        Console.WriteLine("You win again :)");
                }
        }
}
```

As you can see, our hunt for substrings is successful:

```
[hs@localhost mono]$ mono main.exe
You win again :)
```

After that first brief introduction to regular expressions, it's time to have a look at a slightly more complex example:

```
using System;
using System.Text.RegularExpressions;

public class Demo
{
        public static void Main()
        {
                string str = "Sunday Bloody Sunday";

                Regex reg = new Regex("day");
                MatchCollection mat = reg.Matches(str);
                Console.WriteLine("Found: " + mat.Count );

                for     (int i = 0; i < mat.Count; i++)
                {
                        Console.WriteLine("{0} - {1}", i, mat[i]);
                }
        }
}
```

We define a regular expression and look for every match in the string. This time we want all matches to be returned. Therefore, we have to create an instance of the `MatchCollection` object. This class provides many possibilities, but we'll have a look at these features later in this section.

The target of the example is to extract all substrings that match the regular expression and to display them on the screen. In our example, we use a loop to go through the result set.

The next listing shows the result we can expect:

```
[hs@localhost mono]$ mono main.exe
Found: 2
0 - day
1 - day
```

If you don't like `for` loops, you can switch to `foreach` loops. It's necessary to take a closer look at this process because we have to introduce a temporary variable:

```
using System;
using System.Text.RegularExpressions;

public class Demo
{
        public static void Main(string[] args)
```

```
        {
                try
                {
                        foreach (Match mat in Regex.Matches(args[0],
                                args[1]) )
                        {
                                Console.WriteLine( mat );
                        }
                }
                catch
                {
                        Console.WriteLine("Error ...");
                }
        }
}
```

We use the regular expression directly inside the loop and process every value. It is important to know that mat must be an instance of the Match object. Two parameters are passed to Matches. The first parameter contains the string that we want to parse. The second parameter contains the regular expression that has been passed to the program.

In the next listing, you can see how the program works:

```
[hs@localhost mono]$ mono main.exe lalelu l[au]l?
lal
lu
```

Two substrings have been found and displayed on the screen.

Substitutions

Regular expressions cannot be used only for searching and pattern matching. Often regular expressions are used to perform complex substitutions, and that's exactly what we're going to deal with in this section.

Let's get started with a look at an example:

```
using System;
using System.Text.RegularExpressions;

public class Demo
{
        public static void Main(string[] args)
        {
```

```
        try
        {
                Regex reg = new Regex(args[2]);
                string r = reg.Replace(args[0], args[1]);
                Console.WriteLine( r );
        }
        catch (Exception e)
        {
                Console.WriteLine("Error ...");
        }
    }
}
```

First, we define a regular expression. After that, we take the matches and substitute them for the data in the second parameter.

`Replace` needs two strings. All we have to do is tell the method which strings we want to use. When you run the program, the output could look like this:

```
[hs@localhost mono]$ mono main.exe hugohuga paul h.*g
paulopaula
```

Options

Regular expressions provide many features that we haven't dealt with up to now. In this section, it's time to have a closer look at options in general.

Assume that we're looking for a string such as LaTeX. Because it's very likely that only a few people use the correct sequence of lowercase and capitalized letters, we might be in deep trouble. Of course, this problem could be solved with the help of a simple workaround, but as you'll see in the next listing this is definitely not a good idea:

```
(latex)¦(Latex)¦(LAtex)¦(LATex)¦(LATEx)¦(LATEX)¦(lAtex)¦(lATex) ...
```

We check every possible spelling of the word and hope to reach our target that way. This approach would be really slow, so it isn't what we've been looking for. With the help of options, we can tell Mono to perform matching that isn't case sensitive.

In the next example, you can see how this works:

```
using System;
using System.Text.RegularExpressions;

public class Demo
{
```

```
public static void Main(string[] args)
{
        try
        {
                Regex reg = new Regex("latex",
                        RegexOptions.IgnoreCase);
                Match mat = reg.Match("written in LaTex");
                Console.WriteLine("Match: " + mat);
                Console.WriteLine("Position: " + mat.Index);
        }
        catch
        {
                Console.WriteLine("Error ...");
        }
    }
}
```

Again we create a regular expression. However, this time an additional parameter is passed to the constructor, which makes sure that the entire operation is not case sensitive.

When starting the program, the result will look like this:

```
[hs@localhost mono]$ mono main.exe
Match: LaTex
Position: 11
```

Mono provides a rich set of additional options that are essential for implementing high-level applications. The following is a list of the most important settings:

- IgnoreCase: Performs case-insensitive pattern matching.

- Multiline: When you activate this setting, the meanings of ^ and $ will be different.

- ExplicitCapture: Matches must be explicitly marked as groups.

- Compiled: Regular expressions will be precompiled.

- Singleline: The . operator can be used for \n as well.

- IgnorePatternWhitespace: Whitespace characters will be ignored.

- RightToLeft: The expression will be evaluated from right to left.

- ECMAScript: This mode can be activated in combination with IgnoreCase and Multiline.

If you want to turn on more than just one option, you can use the following syntax:

```
Regex reg = new Regex("latex",
        RegexOptions.IgnoreCase | RegexOptions.Multiline |
        RegexOptions.ExplicitCapture|RegexOptions.Compiled |
        RegexOptions.Singleline | RegexOptions.IgnorePatternWhitespace |
        RegexOptions.RightToLeft | RegexOptions.ECMAScript);
```

In this example, we turned on all options. This makes no sense, but it's important for you to see how multiple options can be used.

Precompiled Expressions

If you like, you can tell Mono to precompile a regular expression. In the previous section, you saw that Mono supports an option called Compiled. In this section, you learn what this option does and when you should use it.

A regular expression is normally represented as a sequence of internal commands that are evaluated at runtime. If you mark a regular expression as Compiled, it will be transformed to Microsoft Intermediate Language code directly. At runtime, the MSIL instructions are transformed to native, highly optimized code. This approach is faster. Keep in mind that precompiled code cannot be directly removed by the garbage collection algorithm, so your program will have longer startup times.

Mono Versus .NET

Most of this book is based on Mono 0.23. Not all features of the .NET Framework are fully supported. In older versions of Mono, (for example, 0.15) one of these features was the capability to assign matches to groups. With this feature, you can assign parts of an expression to names.

The following listing shows some code we tested with csc (the .NET compiler) and mcs:

```
using System;
using System.Text.RegularExpressions;

public class Demo
{
        public static void Main(string[] args)
        {
                try
                {
                        Regex q = new Regex(
                                "(?<one>\\w+):(?<two>\\w+)");
```

```
                    Match n = q.Match("Income:3423421");
                    Console.WriteLine("{0} = {1}",
                            n.Groups["one"].Value,
                            n.Groups["two"].Value);
            }
            catch (Exception e)
            {
                    Console.WriteLine("Error ...");
            }
        }
}
```

Inside the regular expression, we define a name that we can use in combination with the Groups method. This leads to the result shown in the next listing:

```
[hs@localhost mono]$ mono main.exe
Income = 3423421
```

If you're still using an old version of Mono, it's possible to use a little workaround to achieve the same target. Here is the code:

```
using System;
using System.Text.RegularExpressions;

public class Demo
{
        public static void Main(string[] args)
    {
        try
            {
                    Regex q = new Regex("(\\w+):(\\w+)");
                    Match n = q.Match("Income:3423421");
                    Console.WriteLine("{0} = {1}",
                            n.Groups[1].Value,
                            n.Groups[2].Value);
            }
            catch (Exception e)
            {
                    Console.WriteLine("Error ...");
            }
        }
}
```

In Brief

- A string is a sequence of characters.

- Mono provides outstanding classes for managing strings.

- One Unicode character needs more than just one byte of storage.

- Strings can be split into an array.

- Regular expressions can be used for parsing strings.

- With regular expressions, you can perform pattern matching.

- Precompiling regular expressions leads to better performance.

Threads

When a program becomes complex, it can happen that the program cannot be managed in one thread any more. Just think of a Web server. Many people want to retrieve data concurrently, so the Web server has to manage many different operations at a time.

In general, there are two ways to implement concurrency. One way is to use multiple processes. The kernel of the operating system makes sure that every process gets enough CPU power and I/O to get the job done. The second way is to have one process doing all the work with the help of threads.

Threads are a good choice to achieve some sort of parallelism because they're fast. This chapter is dedicated to examining threads, so let's get started.

Overview

As we've already mentioned in this book, Mono and .NET provide a rich set of classes. Some of these classes are essential for dealing with threads. The following list provides an overview of the most important components:

- Monitor: Offers mechanisms to manage the access to objects.

- ReaderWriterLock: Implements access to objects. Many objects can read concurrently, but just one instance is allowed to perform write operations.

- RegisteredWaitHandle: Contains a handle for RegisterWaitForSingleObject.

- Thread: Manages and creates a thread.

- ThreadPool: Contains highly developed mechanisms for managing a set of threads.

- **Timer**: Enables you to execute threads in certain intervals.

- **WaitHandle**: Encapsulates system-specific objects that are waiting for unlimited access to an object.

Currently, the Mono framework provides almost all features of the .NET Framework.

Simple Threads

In the following listing, you learn to create and manage simple threads. Let's have a look at the code:

```
using System;
using System.Threading;

class MyThread
{
        static void Main()
        {
                MyThread sth = new MyThread();
                Thread thr = new Thread(new ThreadStart(sth.Message));
                thr.Start();
        }

        public void Message()
        {
                Console.WriteLine("Hello from thread");
        }
}
```

The following example works without explicitly creating an instance of an object:

```
using System;
using System.Threading;

class MyThread
{
        static void Main()
        {
                Thread thr = new Thread(new ThreadStart(Message));
                thr.Start();
        }
```

```
static public void Message()
{
        Console.WriteLine("Hello from thread");
}
}
```

We create a class called MyThread. Inside the Main function, we create an instance of the object itself and pass it to the thread to start an instance of ThreadStart. We can do this with the help of what is called a *delegate*. We've already dealt with delegates earlier in this book.

Finally, we start the thread. The program displays the following piece of text:

```
[hs@localhost mono]$ mono main.exe
Hello from thread
```

Now that you've seen how two threads can be started, it's time to see how two threads can be created. To make the program a bit clearer, we use separate classes so that you can understand the program easily:

```
using System;
using System.Threading;

public class MyThread
{
        public static void Thr1()
        {
                Console.WriteLine("Hello von Thread 1");
        }

        public static void Thr2()
        {
                Console.WriteLine("Hello von Thread 2");
        }
}

public class Demo
{
        public static void Main()
        {
                Thread th1 = new Thread(new ThreadStart(MyThread.Thr1));
                Thread th2 = new Thread(new ThreadStart(MyThread.Thr2));

                th1.Start();
                th2.Start();
        }
}
```

The MyThread class consists of two methods. Two threads are defined inside the Main function. Again we pass an instance of ThreadStart to the constructor. Inside the constructor, we use delegates to define which method should be called. It isn't necessary to use two different methods. It's no problem to use the same method twice.

At the end of the program, we start both threads. The next listing shows the result we can expect. Keep in mind that the order of those two lines is more or less random:

```
[hs@localhost mono]$ mono main.exe
Hello von Thread 1
Hello von Thread 2
```

Every thread displays a message on screen.

Until now, you haven't seen anything new. In the next example, you see how you can make a thread sleep for some amount of time:

```
using System;
using System.Threading;

public class MyThread
{
        public static void Thr()
        {
                for     (int i = 0; i < 3; i++)
                {
                        Thread tr = Thread.CurrentThread;
                        Console.WriteLine("{0}: Thread: {1}",
                                i, tr.Name );
                        Thread.Sleep(1);

                }
        }
}

public class Demo
{
        public static void Main()
        {
                Thread th1 = new Thread(new ThreadStart(MyThread.Thr));
                th1.Name = "Thread 1";

                Thread th2 = new Thread(new ThreadStart(MyThread.Thr));
                th2.Name = "Thread 2";
```

```
        th1.Start();
        th2.Start();
    }
}
```

Let's have a look at the main program first: We create two threads and assign a name to every thread. The advantage of names is that a thread can be identified easily. The behavior of the thread can be defined inside the thread.

In the example, every thread starts the Thr method, which can be found in MyThread. Inside the thread, we ask for its name. With the help of Sleep, you can make a thread sleep for some time and tell the scheduler to continue with another thread. In other words, threads will start working concurrently. The output of the program looks like this:

```
[hs@localhost mono]$ mono main.exe
0: Thread: Thread 1
0: Thread: Thread 2
1: Thread: Thread 1
1: Thread: Thread 2
2: Thread: Thread 1
2: Thread: Thread 2
```

Again, the order of the lines is random. The output can even be interspersed on one line because writing one line is not an atomic operation, so the scheduler might switch to a different thread in the middle of the WriteLine function. In our example, our two threads will be called in rotation.

In case of complex applications, this doesn't help much when all threads sleep for the same time. Therefore, the time that a thread should sleep can be defined. Mono provides a method called TimeSpan, which will help you until a thread wakes up again.

In the next example, you can see how threads can go to sleep and wake up again:

```
using System;
using System.Threading;

public class MyThread
{
        public static void Thr()
        {
                int Hours = 0;
                int Minutes = 0;
                int Seconds = 0;
```

```
          for       (Seconds = 0; Seconds < 3; Seconds++)
          {
                    Thread tr = Thread.CurrentThread;
                    Console.WriteLine("{0}: Thread: {1}",
                            Seconds, tr.Name );
                    TimeSpan SleepTime = new TimeSpan(Hours,
                            Minutes, Seconds);
                    Thread.Sleep(SleepTime);
          }
     }
}


public class Demo
{
     public static void Main()
     {
          Thread th1 = new Thread(new ThreadStart(MyThread.Thr));
          th1.Name = "Thread 1";

          Thread th2 = new Thread(new ThreadStart(MyThread.Thr));
          th2.Name = "Thread 2";

          th1.Start();
          th2.Start();
     }
}
```

The constructor of the object is called with three parameters. The instance returned by the constructor is used and Sleep is called.

The output of the program can be seen in the this listing (still random output):

```
[hs@localhost mono]$ mono main.exe
0: Thread: Thread 1
1: Thread: Thread 1
0: Thread: Thread 2
1: Thread: Thread 2
2: Thread: Thread 1
2: Thread: Thread 2
```

Priorities

Up to now, all threads had the same priority and therefore all threads were called exactly three times. One thread was called after the other. However, sometimes some threads are more important than others because they have to run faster.

In the next example, you can see how different priorities can be assigned to a thread (Thread.Priority has not been fully implemented yet):

```csharp
using System;
using System.Threading;

public class MyThread
{
        public static void Thr()
        {
                for     (int i = 0; i < 3; i++)
                {
                        Thread tr = Thread.CurrentThread;
                        Console.WriteLine("{0} Thread: {1}",
                                i, tr.Name );
                        Thread.Sleep(1);
                }
        }
}

public class Demo
{
        public static void Main()
        {
                Thread th1 = new Thread(new ThreadStart(MyThread.Thr));
                th1.Name = "Thread 1";
                th1.Priority = ThreadPriority.Highest;

                Thread th2 = new Thread(new ThreadStart(MyThread.Thr));
                th2.Name = "Thread 2";
                th2.Priority = ThreadPriority.AboveNormal;

                Thread th3 = new Thread(new ThreadStart(MyThread.Thr));
                th3.Name = "Thread 3";
                th3.Priority = ThreadPriority.Normal;
```

```
              Thread th4 = new Thread(new ThreadStart(MyThread.Thr));
              th4.Name = "Thread 4";
              th4.Priority = ThreadPriority.BelowNormal;

              Thread th5 = new Thread(new ThreadStart(MyThread.Thr));
              th5.Name = "Thread 5";
              th5.Priority = ThreadPriority.Lowest;

              th1.Start();
              th2.Start();
              th3.Start();
              th4.Start();
              th5.Start();
      }
}
```

Five different priorities can be assigned to a thread. The scheduler makes sure that every thread gets the CPU time it needs. In our example, we create five threads so that you can see how different threads compete with each other. In the following listing, you see the result you can expect. Keep in mind that the result might differ on your machine:

```
[hs@duron threads]$ mono prio.exe
0 Thread: Thread 2
0 Thread: Thread 4
0 Thread: Thread 3
0 Thread: Thread 5
0 Thread: Thread 1
1 Thread: Thread 2
1 Thread: Thread 4
1 Thread: Thread 3
1 Thread: Thread 5
1 Thread: Thread 1
2 Thread: Thread 2
2 Thread: Thread 4
2 Thread: Thread 3
2 Thread: Thread 5
2 Thread: Thread 1
```

When working with threads, you have to take into consideration that the order in which threads are called is not deterministic. The output depends on the scheduler.

Locking and Synchronization

When threads compete with each other, each thread tries to get enough hardware resources. This can easily lead to troubles, so it's necessary to find solutions for this problem. In this section, we have a look at the most basic algorithms for working with threads safely. Because threading is a complex subject, we deal with only the very basics. However, for most applications, we provide enough information.

Locking

Locking is an interesting yet complex issue. Let's get started with an example:

```
using System;
using System.Threading;

public class Demo
{
        public int data = 0;

        public static void Main()
        {
                Demo MyDemo = new Demo();
                Thread th1 = new Thread(
                        new ThreadStart(MyDemo.CalcAndReport));
                th1.Name = "Thread 1";

                Thread th2 = new Thread(
                        new ThreadStart(MyDemo.CalcAndReport));
                th2.Name = "Thread 2";

                th1.Start();
                th2.Start();

        }

        public void CalcAndReport()
        {
                for     (int i = 0; i < 4; i++)
                {
                        Thread tr = Thread.CurrentThread;
                        lock    (this)
                        {
```

```
                        data++;
                        Console.WriteLine("{0}: {1}",
                                tr.Name, data);
                }
                Thread.Sleep(1);
        }
    }
}
```

In this example, our class contains one attribute. Whenever you want to write an application where more than just one thread tries to access this variable, we must protect it. In our example, this isn't that important. But when it comes to more complex applications, this will be essential. Locking will be a key issue you have to deal with properly and carefully to make sure that accessing resources concurrently does not lead to troubles. But let's get back to the code we just saw: In the Main function, two threads are created. The CalcAndReport method is used as a delegate. This method does nothing more than increment the value of our class's attributes. As you can see, we define a lock to make sure that only one thread can access this variable at once. The only thing you have to do is find out which data has to be locked. In our example, the current object is locked.

In the next listing, you can see which result Mono returns:

```
[hs@localhost mono]$ mono main.exe
Thread 1: 1
Thread 2: 2
Thread 1: 3
Thread 2: 4
Thread 1: 5
Thread 2: 6
Thread 2: 7
Thread 1: 8
```

If the attribute of our class is not locked, the output might look like this:

```
[hs@duron threads]$ mono prio.exe
Thread 2: 2
Thread 1: 1
Thread 2: 3
Thread 1: 4
Thread 2: 5
Thread 1: 6
Thread 2: 7
Thread 1: 8
```

As you can see, the numbers are not returned in the same order.

It can get even worse than this: Without the lock, the final value could easily reach 8 because of a race condition in which one thread reads and updates the value, but before it can store the new value in data, the other thread reads the old value. This can be a real problem because sometimes threads must be in synch.

Synchronization and Mutexes

When working with threads, one of the most important things to consider is that threads must be able to block each other. In modern literature about threading, this is called *mutual exclusion* (or *mutex*, for short). A mutex can be held by exactly one thread at a time. If two threads try to lock a mutex at the same time, one thread will be blocked until the thread in charge or the mutex releases the lock. A mutex is normally used to protect data that's accessed by more than just one thread. It's important to know that a mutex is always global. That's necessary because it must be seen by all threads that a program consists of. Otherwise, the concept would not make too much sense. For a programmer, it is important to define what a mutex is supposed to protect. Using a mutex is often a good idea to serialize access to objects.

C# provides a set of classes so that you can manage mutexes efficiently and easy. In this section, we see how these classes can be used and how software based on mutexes can be implemented. Let's start with a simple example:

```csharp
using System;
using System.Threading;

public class Demo
{
        static Mutex mut;

        public static void Main()
        {
                mut = new Mutex(true);
                Demo a = new Demo();

                Thread t= new Thread(new ThreadStart(a.Method));
                t.Start();

                Console.WriteLine("before");
                Thread.Sleep(1000);
                Console.WriteLine("after");
                mut.ReleaseMutex();
                Console.WriteLine("end");
        }
```

```
public void Method()

{
        Console.WriteLine("Start");
        mut.WaitOne( );
        Console.WriteLine("End");
}
}
```

At the beginning of the program, we create an instance of the Mutex object. The parameter passed to the constructor tells the system whether the calling thread is the owner of the mutex. After creating an instance of Demo, we start a thread. Then we see what happens when text is displayed and the mutex is released.

The next listing shows the result we can expect:

```
[hs@localhost mono]$ mono main.exe
Start
before
after
end
End
```

As you can see, the mutex makes sure that the order in which the code is executed is correct.

The Mutex class is extremely important. Therefore, we've decided to list the most important overloadings of the constructor here:

- Mutex()

- Mutex(boolean)

- Mutex(boolean, string)

- Mutex(boolean, string, boolean)

The second parameter can be used to assign a name to the thread. With the help of the third parameter, it's possible to define the rights of the thread.

After that overview of the constructors provided by Mono, let's take a look at the most important methods:

- Close: Deletes a mutex and releases all locks.

- ReleaseMutex: Releases a mutex.

- WaitOne: Blocks the current thread. This method is one of the most essential features provided by this class.

In Brief

- Parallel execution can be implemented with threads.

- Threads can be synchronized with each other to avoid conflicts.

- Different priorities can be assigned to a thread.

- Mono does not currently support priorities.

- To avoid race conditions, locks must be used.

- Mutexes are used to synchronize threads and to perform mutual exclusion.

- Synchronizing threads is all about locking and waiting.

Network Programming

10

IN THIS CHAPTER

- **Fundamentals**
- **Socket Programming**
- WebRequest
- **DNS**
- **In Brief**

The ability to transfer data from one place to another is not new. In the 19th century, Alexander Graham Bell was the first to transmit sounds over a cable. Just a few people understood the importance of that invention. A well-known newspaper even published that well-informed people knew that transmitting data with the help of a cable was completely useless. Times have changed and now it's almost impossible to imagine a world without digital transmission of data.

In this chapter, we take a closer look at network programming. You'll see how network-based applications can be implemented with the help of Mono.

Fundamentals

In this section, we examine the fundamentals of network programming.

Protocols

When data is transmitted over a network, you need what are known as protocols. In most cases, TCP/IP (Transmission Control Protocol/Internet Protocol) is considered to be the state of the art. However, TCP/IP is not just a simple protocol. In reality, it is a rich set of protocols and each of these protocols has a specific task. There are also other protocols, such as the good old IPX/SPX, but those protocols are no longer in widespread use.

In general, two different types or protocols are available: connection-oriented protocols and non-connection-oriented protocols.

Connection-Oriented Protocols

Connection-oriented protocols are a good way to exchange data reliably. Before the actual data is transmitted, the client and the server perform a handshake. If that process is successful, a connection is established. Establishing a connection leads to some overhead, but it leads to higher security and higher reliability. When using a connection-oriented protocol, it's rather unlikely that packets will be lost (depending on the quality of the line, of course) because the network stack will make sure that missing data is retransmitted again. When transmitting data over the Internet, it can happen that packets overtake each other; it is in no way guaranteed that a packet that has been sent first will be the first one to reach the client. The TCP stack of the operating system makes sure that the packets received from the network are brought back into the right order again. If a packet gets lost, the operating system requests the missing data again.

TCP is a connection-oriented protocol, but we'll get back to that again later in this chapter.

Non-Connection-Oriented Protocols

Protocols that are not connection oriented are faster to set up than connection-oriented ones. The reason is because there isn't that much overhead. However, the problem is that the server does not know whether the client has received a packet because there's no connection between the server and the client. Again, it is possible for packets to overtake each other, so the client has to order the packet.

UDP (User Datagram Protocol) is the most widely known protocol that does not rely on connections. We'll get back to UDP in a moment.

Sockets

Sockets are a fundamental component of network programming—they're an abstraction layer between the low-level communication mechanisms and the programmer. The kernel provides the correct data to the programmer via a socket.

The basic idea is to hide a major part of the complexity of the communication between client and server from the user who does not have to care about things such as packets overtaking each other, packet sizes, and so forth. All those things are managed by the operating system.

As you can easily imagine, sockets are an important feature of every modern operating system.

Socket Programming

After this first theoretical overview, let's move on to look at the Mono framework and see how sockets can be used. Although a lot of effort is put into *n*-tier applications, classical client/server applications are still widely used.

As you know, client/server applications consist of two processes. The server process provides data for the client. The server processes requests and returns the results. In most practical applications, a server is supposed to process requests concurrently.

In this section, we examine how simple server and client applications can be implemented.

Simple TCP Servers

We start with a simple scenario. The server waits for data and terminates as soon as data is received.

```
using System;
using System.Net.Sockets;
using System.Text;

class MyServer
{
        public MyServer(int port)
        {
                Byte[] inBuffer = new Byte[256];
                int cnt;
                string MyData = "";

                ASCIIEncoding ASCII = new ASCIIEncoding();
                TcpListener MyLsrn = new TcpListener(port);
                MyLsrn.Start();

                try
                {
                        Socket MySock = MyLsrn.AcceptSocket();
                        cnt = MySock.Receive(inBuffer,
                                inBuffer.Length, 0);

                        MyData = ASCII.GetString(inBuffer, 0, cnt);
                        Console.WriteLine("DEBUG: " + MyData);

                        if      (MyData.Trim() == "end")
```

```
            {
                    Console.WriteLine("The end is near");
            }
            else
            {
                    Console.WriteLine("The end :(");
            }
        }
        catch (Exception e)
        {
                Console.WriteLine("Error: " + e.Message );
        }

        MyLsrn.Stop();
    }
}

class Demo
{
    public static void Main()
    {
        MyServer srv = new MyServer(10000);
    }
}
```

The program contains two classes. Demo contains a sample application and creates an instance of MyServer. The port that the server should listen to is passed to the constructor as a parameter.

The MyServer class is a bit more complex. At the beginning of the constructor, we define some variables that we'll need later on in the program. An instance of ASCIIEncoding is generated. This object is important because we'll use it to extract the data that the client has sent us. With the help of objects such as ASCIIEncoding, we can define which encoding our server should use.

After that, a listener is created. The port we've passed to the constructor is passed to TcpListener. Now we bind the listener to a socket. The socket is fundamental for the entire process because all data we're going to send and receive is sent through the socket.

Let's have a look at the Receive method you can use for reading from the socket. In our example, the method is called with three parameters. The first one contains the buffer we want to add the data to. The second parameter informs Mono about the size of the data we want to read. With the help of the third parameter, we define the position at which we want to start adding data to the buffer.

For displaying the data in the buffer, we convert it to a string. Depending on the data we receive from the client, a string is sent to standard output. Finally, we terminate the listener.

The easiest way to test the server is to use good old Telnet. Telnet can be used to show how the communication between a server and a client works. It's possible to transmit data to the server—no server-specific client application is necessary. In our case, we connect to port 10000 and send a string to the server:

```
[hs@duron hs]$ telnet localhost 10000
Trying 127.0.0.1...
Connected to duron (127.0.0.1).
Escape character is '^]'.
this is a lousy process ...
Connection closed by foreign host.
```

As soon as the server receives data, it terminates. That's the way we defined it in the program. It's important to see that we don't have to think about the basics of network communication because most of the work has already been done by the operating system. This makes the entire work incredibly simple.

Simple TCP Clients

To make sure that the server we just implemented has the right counterpart, we implement a client application:

```csharp
using System;
using System.IO;
using System.Net;
using System.Text;
using System.Net.Sockets;

public class clnt
{
        public static void Main()
        {
                try {
                        TcpClient MyClient = new TcpClient();
                        MyClient.Connect("127.0.0.1", 10000);

                        String str = "I am a string";
                        Stream stm = MyClient.GetStream();

                        ASCIIEncoding ascii= new ASCIIEncoding();
                        byte[] barray = ascii.GetBytes(str);
```

```
                    stm.Write(barray, 0, barray.Length);

                    byte[] carray = new byte[100];
                    int k = stm.Read(carray, 0, 100);

                    for (int i = 0; i < k; i++)
                    {
                            Console.Write(Convert.ToChar(carray[i]));
                    }

                    MyClient.Close();
            }

            catch (Exception e)
            {
                    Console.WriteLine("Error: " + e.Message);
            }
        }
}
```

At the beginning of the program, a TCP client is started. We use this client to connect to the server. In our example, we connect to the local server that's listening to port 10000. In addition, we define the string that should be transmitted. To transmit the string, we assign a stream to the server. Finally, we write the string into the stream. At the end of the program, we display the content of the array we're using.

When compiling and running the program, the result will be as follows:

```
[hs@localhost mono]$ mono client.exe
Error: Connection refused
```

The client won't connect to the server because this process has not been started yet:

```
[root@duron networking]# mono server.exe &
[1] 18384
[root@duron networking]# mono client.exe
DEBUG: I am a string
The end :(
[1]+  Done                    mono server.exe
```

The desired output will be displayed.

Bi-directional TCP Servers

Up to now, you've learned to write simple client/server applications that do nothing other than display simple text on the screen. However, servers that have to fulfill very special tasks must be able to perform some additional duties. The server has to process the requests received from clients, and must find the right answer to a certain request. In this section, we take a look at a more complex example so that you can see how advanced servers can be implemented with the help of Mono.

Let's start with the server process again. Keep in mind that it is a prototype showing how things should work—this is not a complete application:

```
using System;
using System.Net.Sockets;
using System.Text;

class MyServer
{
        public MyServer(int port)
        {
                Byte[] auth = new Byte[256];
                string status = "start";
                int cnt;
                string MyData;

                ASCIIEncoding ASCII = new ASCIIEncoding();
                TcpListener MyLsrn = new TcpListener(port);
                MyLsrn.Start();

                do
                {
                        try
                        {
                                Socket sk = MyLsrn.AcceptSocket();
                                cnt = sk.Receive(auth,
                                        auth.Length, 0);

                                MyData = ASCII.GetString(auth, 0, cnt);
                                Console.WriteLine("({0}) - {1}",
                                        MyData.Length, MyData);

                                if      (MyData == "start"
                                        && status == "start")
```

```
                              {
                                          Console.WriteLine("Startup");
                                          sk.Send(ASCII.GetBytes("ok"));
                                          status = "ok";
                              }
                              if      (MyData == "ok")
                              {
                                          // Processing requests ...
                              }
                              if      (MyData == "end")
                              {
                                          // Terminate program
                                          Console.WriteLine("End ...");
                                          sk.Send(ASCII.GetBytes("ciao"));
                                          status = "end";
                              }
                    }
                    catch (Exception e)
                    {
                              Console.WriteLine("Error: "
                                          + e.Message );
                    }
            } while (status != "end");

            MyLsrn.Stop();
        }
}


class Demo
{
        public static void Main()
        {
              MyServer srv = new MyServer(10000);
        }
}
```

At the beginning of the program, we define four variables. The first one contains the data we receive from the client. All data that is transmitted to the server will be stored in an array of bytes. This is important because network traffic is based on bytes representing the binary transmission of data. status defines the status of our application. Depending on its content, the server performs certain operations. To display the data in the byte array, we convert it to a string. That can be done with the help of a temporary variable. In our example, this variable is called MyData.

After we create an instance of ASCIIEncoding and a listener, we enter a loop. This loop is executed as long as the status of the application does not tell us that it should be terminated. Inside the loop, you can see that the server behaves differently depending on the status of the application. Based on a simple If statement, we find out which data the client has sent us and adjust the behavior of the server.

The behavior of clients and server is clearly defined by protocols. If you're interested in protocols, we recommend taking a look at the description of the PostgreSQL front end/back end protocol at http://www.postgresql.org/idocs/index.php?protocol.html. The document you can find there shows what a protocol can look like and how things work. Because of the excellent documentation, PostgreSQL is a good example and is easy to find your way through.

Let's get back to our server process. The main idea of the example is bi-directional communication. To send data to the server, you can call the Send method. You must keep in mind that the data has to be provided as an array of bytes. To convert a string to a byte array, you can call GetStrings for an instance of the ASCIIEncoding object.

After implementing the server, it's time to have a look at the client application. Implementing clients is much easier than working on server applications. In our case, we want to implement a client that communicates with our server process. Let's start with some code:

```
using System;
using System.IO;
using System.Net;
using System.Text;
using System.Net.Sockets;

public class clnt
{
        public static void Main()
        {
                TcpClient MyClient = new TcpClient();
                MyClient.Connect("127.0.0.1", 10000);

                String str = "start";
                Stream stm = MyClient.GetStream();

                try
                {
                        ASCIIEncoding ascii= new ASCIIEncoding();
                        byte[] barray = ascii.GetBytes(str);
```

```
            stm.Write(barray, 0, barray.Length);

            byte[] carray = new byte[100];
            int k = stm.Read(carray, 0, 100);
            str = ascii.GetString(carray);

            // Checking the return value
            if      (str == "ok")
            {
                    Console.WriteLine("Authentication ok");

                    // additional interaction
            }
            if      (str == "whatever ...")
            {
                    // do something
            }

            MyClient.Close();
        }

        catch (Exception e)
        {
                Console.WriteLine("Error: " + e.Message);
        }
    }
}
```

At the beginning of the program, we create a TCP client. Again, we create a stream that we'll need for communicating. Just as when implementing a server, it is necessary to find the correct answer to the message of the remote machine. As you can see, our prototype uses a simple If statement to find out what to do next. The test if(str=="ok") doesn't work on either the latest Mono or on .NET 1.1. The problem is that when you call str=ascii.GetString(carray); the length of str becomes 100 (the length of the carray.) The length of ok is 2, and the string equality operator returns false if the string lengths are different.

To start the two programs as a team, you can use the information provided in the next listing:

```
[root@duron networking]# mono server.exe &
[1] 19014
[root@duron networking]# mono client.exe
```

```
(5) - start
Startup
Authentication ok
```

Both the client and the server display messages on the screen. In case of practical applications, it's useful to use log files for that purpose.

Servers and Multithreading

Until now, a server had exactly one connection to exactly one client. For practical examples, this isn't the way it is supposed to be because many clients should be able to access the server concurrently. Therefore, it's necessary that one server consist of many processes or a set of threads to ensure that enough clients can be connected at a time.

In case of Mono, threaded servers are the right approach to take. In classical Unix applications, multiple processes are used instead of threads. Many readers will know this concept from the Apache 1.x server. Servers consisting of many processes are based on forking. In forking, a main process handles a set of child processes. Each of those processes communicates with one client. Whenever a new client establishes a connection to the server, a new child process is created. To raise the performance of an application, it's even possible to keep a set of processes in memory. Architectures based on forking are reliable because if one process dies the rest of the server is not affected. Alternatively, nonblocking I/O using select() and poll() can be used in a single-threaded process.

C# propagates a different concept: A server process should rely on threads and everything should be running on one process. In most cases, threads are faster than managing various processes, so this is an advantage over forking servers.

In this book, we've already dealt with threads extensively. In the next few sections, we look at the basic classes you'll need to implement servers and clients. These classes are essential because they do most of the work.

TcpListener—The Details

The TcpListener class can be used to wait for incoming connections. Various constructors are provided:

- TcpListener(Int32): Defines the port to which a listener should listen.

- TcpListener(IPEndPoint): The listener is supposed to listen to a certain IP address. IPEndPoint encapsulates the IP address and port tuple in a single object.

- TcpListener(IPAddress, Int32): The listener listens to an IP address making use of a special port.

In addition, the following methods are provided:

- AcceptSocket: Accepts a pending connection.

- AcceptTcpClient: Accepts a pending connection.

- Finalize: Frees all resources. This method should not be used by the programmer because it is used behind the scenes by the runtime.

- Pending: Tries to find out whether a waiting connection exists.

- Start: Starts to listen to a connection.

- Stop: Stops listening to a connection.

TcpClient—**The Details**

The TcpClient object is the counterpart of TcpListener. It's designed to communicate with a server. The constructor has been overloaded several times:

- TcpClient(): Creates a basic instance

- TcpClient(IPEndPoint): Defines a server to talk to

- TcpClient(String, Int32): Establishes a connection to a server listening to a certain port

The following methods are essential:

- Close(): Terminates a connection

- Connect(IPEndPoint): Establishes a connection to a remote server

- Connect(IPAddress, Int32): Establishes a connection to a certain host/port

- Connect(String, Int32): Establishes a connection to a certain host/port

- Dispose: Frees resources

- Finalize: Frees resources (should not be used by the programmer)

- GetStream: Returns the stream that's used for sending and receiving data

The TcpClient object provides some properties that are essential for your daily work. With the help of those variables, it's easy to retrieve information about an instance and implement highly sophisticated applications.

The following list contains an overview of the most important variables:

- `LingerState`: Defines the time a socket is allowed to linger

- `NoDelay`: Defines latency times

- `ReceiveBufferSize`: Defines the size of the buffer storing incoming data

- `ReceiveTimeout`: Sets the timeout for incoming data (not supported by the Linux kernel)

- `SendBufferSize`: Defines the buffer for outgoing data

- `SendTimeout`: Defines the timeout for outgoing data (not supported by the Linux kernel)

Socket—The Details

The `Socket` object is the central component of the Mono framework when it comes to networking. In this section, we take a closer look at the `Socket` object and see what features this class provides.

The constructor has the following syntax:

```
Socket(AddressFamily, SocketType, ProtocolType)
```

The preceding constructor creates a socket and accepts a set of parameters.

The list of methods of the `Socket` object is long and provides everything you need. The following list contains the most important methods:

- `Accept`: Accepts an incoming connection.

- `BeginAccept`: Opens an asynchronous connection.

- `BeginConnect`: Establishes an asynchronous connection.

- `BeginReceive`: Starts reading data from an asynchronous connection.

- `BeginReceiveFrom`: Starts reading data from a specific asynchronous connection.

- `BeginSend`: Sends data across an asynchronous connection.

- `BeginSendTo`: Sends data to a specific destination (asynchronous connection).

- `Bind`: Binds a socket to a local resource.

- `Close`: Closes a socket.

- `Connect`: Establishes an asynchronous connection.

- `Dispose`: Frees resources.

- `EndAccept`: Terminates an asynchronous connection.

- `EndConnect`: Terminates an asynchronous connection.

- `EndReceive`: Stops receiving data.

- `EndReceiveFrom`: Stops receiving data from a specific data source.

- `EndSend`: Stops sending data.

- `EndSendTo`: Stops sending data to a specific target.

- `Finalize`: Frees resources.

- `Listen`: Sets the status to "listen."

- `Poll`: Retrieves the status of the socket.

- `Receive(Byte[])`: Reads data into an array of bytes.

- `Receive(Byte[], SocketFlags)`: Reads data into an array of bytes.

- `Receive(Byte[], Int32, SocketFlags)`: Reads a certain amount of data into an array of bytes.

- `Receive(Byte[], Int32, Int32, SocketFlags)`: Reads a certain amount of data into an array of bytes. The second parameter defines an offset inside the array of bytes. The third parameter tells Mono how much data it has to copy.

- `Select`: Asks for the status of one or more sockets.

- `Send(Byte[])`: Sends data.

- `Send(Byte[], SocketFlags)`: Sends data.

- `Send(Byte[], Int32, SocketFlags)`: Sends data and defines the length of the data that should be sent.

- `Send(Byte[], Int32, Int32, SocketFlags)`: Sends data. The starting position inside the array and the amount of data that should be transmitted can be defined.

- `SendTo`: Sends data to a specific host.

- `SendTo(Byte[], SocketFlags)`: Sends data to a specific host.

- `SendTo(Byte[], Int32, SocketFlags)`: Sends data to a specific host and defines the length of the data that should be sent.

- `SendTo(Byte[], Int32, Int32, SocketFlags)`: Sends data to a specific host. The starting position inside the array and the amount of data that should be transmitted can be defined.

- `SetSocketOption(SocketOptionLevel, SocketOptionName, Byte[])`: Defines parameters of a socket.

- `SetSocketOption(SocketOptionLevel, SocketOptionName, Int32)`: Defines parameters of a socket.

- `SetSocketOption(SocketOptionLevel, SocketOptionName, Object)`: Defines parameters of a socket.

- `Shutdown(how)`: Tells a socket that sending and transmitting ends.

The connection dealt with by the `Begin/End` methods is no different from the connection dealt with by the other methods. The connection itself is not asynchronous, but the method call is. Sockets have a set of properties. Let's have a look at an overview:

- `AddressFamily`: Returns the address family

- `Available`: Returns the amount of data that can be returned

- `Blocking`: Tells us whether the server blocks

- `Connected`: Tells us whether the socket is connected to a remote data source

- `Handle`: Contains a system handle

- `LocalEndPoint`: Contains the local end point

- `ProtocolType`: Returns the type of the protocol

- `RemoteEndPoint`: Contains the remote end point

- `SocketType`: Returns the type of the socket

SocketException—The Details

Mono provides a class for managing errors returned by sockets. This class is important because it will help you keep track of what's going wrong during your network communication. This section features a brief look at `SocketException`. Let's get started with a look at the constructors:

- `SocketException()`: Creates an instance

- `SocketException(Int32)`: Creates an instance of the object and accepts an error code

- `SocketException(SerializationInfo, StreamContext)`: Creates an instance that's based on `SerializationInfo` and `StreamingContent`

In the case of the SocketException object, properties are extremely important because they contain the desired information. Let's see which possibilities are available:

- ErrorCode: Contains an error code

- HelpLink: Contains a link to a page explaining the error

- InnerException: Creates an instance of the Exception object

- Message: Contains an error message

- NativeErrorCode: Returns a Win32 error code

- Source: Returns the name of the application that caused the error

- StackTrace: Returns a string representation of the stack

- TargetSite: Returns the method causing the error

WebRequest

Sockets are fundamental when data should be transmitted over a network. They're the most basic component that can be accessed by a C# programmer. That implies that talking to sockets is too complex for the most common tasks. Therefore, Mono provides a set of classes to help you use the most common protocols.

The Web has become an important component of our everyday life. Therefore, requesting Web sites is a basic operation. With the help of WebRequest, it's possible to retrieve the content of a Web site.

HTTP

This section takes a closer look at HTTP (Hypertext Transfer Protocol). We start with an example in which you can see how data can be loaded from a Web server:

```
using System;
using System.Net;
using System.IO;
using System.Text;

public class MyWget
{
        public MyWget(string url)
        {
                try
                {
```

```
                ASCIIEncoding ASCII = new ASCIIEncoding();
                WebRequest request = WebRequest.Create(url);
                WebResponse response = request.GetResponse();

                StreamReader reader = new
                StreamReader(response.GetResponseStream(), ASCII);

                string str = reader.ReadLine();
                while(str != null)
                {
                        Console.WriteLine(str);
                        str = reader.ReadLine();
                }
            }
            catch (Exception e)
            {
                    Console.WriteLine("Error: " + e.Message);
                    Console.WriteLine("Method: " + e.TargetSite);
                    Console.WriteLine("Stack: " + e.StackTrace);
            }
        }
    }


public class Demo
{
        public static void Main()
        {
                MyWget cybertec = new MyWget("http://www.cybertec.at");
        }
}
```

Before we present this example in detail, we want to admit that this example works on Windows as long as you are using Mono 0.15. It seems as if this version has a bug in the asynchronous delegates. In more recent versions of Mono, that bug has been fixed and the example compiles and runs on every platform.

Let's get back to the code.

At the beginning of the program, we create an encoding. After that, we create an instance of WebRequest and WebResponse. When creating the WebRequest, we pass the URL of the site we want to call to Create. To create the WebResponse object, we call the GetResponse method. To extract the data from the WebResponse object, we need a method called GetResponseStream. Displaying the data on screen is an easy task because we can take the string and use WriteLine.

If an error occurs, our application will catch it because we implemented a `try/catch` mechanism.

In the `Main` function itself, we do nothing other than call `MyWget`. When we start the program, the content of the Web site is displayed.

FTP

FTP (File Transfer Protocol) is one of the most popular protocols available. FTP is an efficient way to transfer data across networks. Just like many other protocols in the TCP/IP family, FTP is an old protocol. It was invented in 1971 and is still widely used around the globe. Well, some good things will live forever. However, in Mono, .NET, and C#, FTP does not play an important role. There are no classes providing support for FTP. If you're looking for FTP support, you can use one of the free implementations of the protocol you can find on the Internet.

We won't deal with these implementations in detail because they are far beyond the scope of this book.

FileWebRequest

If you want to read a file you can use the `FileWebRequest` class. It's a subclass of `WebRequest` and inherits all methods from the parent class. Because `FileWebRequest` works just like the parent class, there's no need to take a closer look at it.

DNS

For many years, DNS has been used to build a bridge between names and IP addresses. Because names are more comfortable than IP addresses, DNS has always been an important protocol. Just imagine if every site on the Web had to be accessed via an IP address—I guess the Internet would not be what it is today. DNS is supported by Mono and .NET, so working with the protocol is an easy task.

In the next example, we present a small example in which you can see how IP addresses can be translated to names:

```
using System;
using System.Net;

public class Demo
{
        public static int Main (string [] args)
        {
```

```
IPAddress dnsip;
if      (args.Length == 0)
{
        Console.WriteLine("Not valid");
        return 1;
}
else
{
        try
        {
                dnsip = IPAddress.Parse(args[0]);
        }
        catch (Exception e)
        {
                Console.WriteLine("Error: {0}",
                        e.Message);
                return 1;
        }
}

IPHostEntry ipEntry;
try
{
        ipEntry = Dns.GetHostByAddress (dnsip);
}
catch (Exception e)
{
        Console.WriteLine("IP: {0}",dnsip);
        Console.WriteLine("Cannot assign value: {0}",
                e.Message);
        return 1;
}

Console.WriteLine ("Hostname: {0}", ipEntry.HostName);
return 0;
        }
}
```

At the beginning of the program, a variable is defined. We use IPAddress as a data type so that we can store the IP address we want to resolve. If an input parameter has been passed to the program, we start transforming it to an IP address. For that purpose, we use a method called Parse. To make sure that nothing can go wrong, we implement a try/catch mechanism.

After we extract the IP address, we try to resolve it. Therefore, we create an instance of the IPHostEntry object. If the name can be resolved, we try to do it. Finally, the output is displayed on the screen:

```
[hs@duron tmp]$ mono dnsip.exe 62.116.21.146
Host Name: scanshopper.postgresql.at
```

Now that you've seen how a corresponding name can be found, let's try to find the IP address for a given name. Examine the following piece of code and see how it works:

```
using System;
using System.Net;

public class Demo
{
        public static int Main (string [] args)
        {
                String strHostName;
                if      (args.Length == 0)
                {
                        Console.WriteLine ("undefined parameter");
                        return 1;
                }
                else
                {
                        strHostName = args[0];
                }

                IPHostEntry ipEntry = Dns.GetHostByName (strHostName);
                IPAddress[] addr = ipEntry.AddressList;

                for (int i = 0; i < addr.Length; i++)
                {
                        Console.WriteLine ("IP Address {0}: {1} ",
                                i, addr[i].ToString ());
                }
                return 0;
        }
}
```

At the beginning of the program, we read an input parameter. If no parameter has been passed to the program, we quit the process. Otherwise, an instance of IPHostEntry is created. We take the instance and assign an IP address to it. It's important to mention that

`AddressList` returns an array having the type `IPAddress`. We'll use this array at the end of the program.

The output of our program might look like this:

```
[hs@duron tmp]$ mono dnsname.exe www.sapdb.at
IP Address 0: 62.116.21.146
```

In this case, we have found out what IP hides behind `www.sapdb.at`.

After that brief introduction, we can have a look at `Dns`. In the following list, we've compiled a set of the most important methods provided by Mono:

- `BeginGetHostByName`: Starts an asynchronous request (`IPHostEntry`)

- `BeginResolve`: Starts resolving DNS information

- `EndGetHostByName`: Terminates an asynchronous request

- `GetHostByAddress`: Returns the IP address of a given host

- `GetHostByName`: Returns the name of a given IP address

- `GetHostName`: Returns the name of the local machine

- `Resolve`: Resolves DNS information

The `Dns` object does not provide properties.

In Brief

- Mono provides advanced features for implementing networks.

- Sockets are fundamental for communicating over a TCP/IP network.

- Mono provides interfaces to sockets as well as to high-level protocols.

- HTTP, FTP, DNS, and so forth are high-level interfaces based on sockets.

- TCP/IP provides connection-oriented (for example, TCP) and non-connection-oriented protocols (for example, UDP).

- Streams are used to send and receive data.

- Not all classes proposed by the .NET Framework are fully implemented yet.

Security

11

IN THIS CHAPTER

- The .NET Security Concept
- Mono and Security
- In Brief

Security is a key issue when it comes to professional and business-critical applications. A few years ago, security was a topic nobody seemed to care about. But because of enhanced networking technologies, more and more computers were connected to networks and so security became an important topic. Back in the early days, there were not as many hackers around as there are nowadays. Important Web sites are attacked more than once a day, and network administrators are responsible for making their sites more secure. It's necessary to monitor and to update a system constantly to make sure that nothing evil happens.

But security is more than just something that has to do with network administration. Programmers have to be careful when writing applications. They have to make sure that their applications are secure and cannot be hacked or used as a weapon against others.

In this chapter, we take a look at security in general. We'll examine the concepts that have been invented to make your Mono application more secure.

The .NET Security Concept

For .NET, Microsoft has designed a completely new concept, which seems to be unique. The new concept is called *code-based security*. The idea behind the concept is comparatively simple, yet powerful: Certain components are allowed to perform certain tasks. In terms of networks, this makes sense because people use components from many different vendors.

Mono does not currently support most of the features we describe in this chapter, but it's important to have at least an impression of what we'll see in upcoming releases of Mono. We examine the key features proposed by Microsoft so that you can see what we can expect from Mono.

The concept proposed by Microsoft and .NET consists of four core components:

- Evidence
- Permissions
- Code Groups
- Security Policy Levels

In the next sections, we take a closer look at each of those components.

Evidence

This information is used to find out which permissions an assembly has. The .NET Framework supports seven different kinds:

- Application Directory: Path to the application
- Hash: MD5 or SHA1 code
- Publisher: Signature of publisher
- Site: Web site where the software can be found
- Strong Name: The name of the assembly
- URL: URL where the software can be found
- Zone: Zone the software comes from

Permissions

The .NET Framework provides a set of different rights:

- Nothing: No rights
- Execution: Can be executed
- Internet: Can be executed when the origin of the software is unknown
- Local Intranet: Enterprise permissions
- Everything: All rights except security checks
- Full Trust: No restrictions

Code Groups

All assemblies are organized in code groups that are organized hierarchically. Permissions can be set based on code groups.

Security Policy Levels

After grouping and assigning rights to assemblies, they can be assigned to security policy levels. .NET supports four levels:

- Enterprise: Managed code that belongs to a company
- Machine: Managed code on the local machine
- User: Managed code that belongs to a user on the local machine
- Application Domain: Managed code that belongs to an applications

Rights

An assembly can have only a subset of a security policy. In general, there are declarative and imperative types. However, in this section, we do not deal with these details. Instead, we have a look at a list of the rights provided by .NET:

- Environment: Read and write environment variables
- FileDialog: Read files
- FileIO: Read and write files
- IsolatedStorage: Access control and generic isolated storage
- IsolatedStorageFile: Access control and virtual file system
- Principal: Role-based security checks
- PublisherIdentity: Access to the code provided by a specific software vendor
- Reflection: Permission to make use of C# reflections
- Registry: Permission to access the registry of the system
- Security: Accessible rights
- SiteIdentity: Permission to access software that can be found on a certain Web site
- StrongName: Permission to access an assembly that has a specific strong name
- UI: User interface and clipboard
- URL: Permission to access local software and software that can be found on the Web
- Zone: Permission to access software in a certain zone

Mono and Security

In the near future, Mono will provide a fully .NET-compliant security concept. In the version of Mono this book is based on, only a few versions of basic classes are available, so it isn't possible to present real code yet. We hope that this will change soon. Because Mono is still in an early state, we've chosen not to include examples yet.

Currently, we do not recommend using the security mechanisms provided by Mono.

In Brief

- .NET proposes advanced security concepts.

- .NET provides various levels of security.

- .NET provides a set of permissions that can be used to make your code more secure.

- Mono does not provide code-based security yet.

- .NET security will most likely not be implemented into Mono in the near future.

Working with Dates and Times

Working with dates and times is an extremely important subject matter that every programmer will face often. In many areas, working with dates and times is essential. Because performing basic operations with dates and times is so fundamental, we've decided to dedicate an entire chapter to the basics and some advanced features of Mono and dealing with dates.

Mono, Dates, and Times

Just like the .NET Framework, Mono provides several classes for dealing with dates and times. In this section, we take a closer look at the fundamentals you should be familiar with.

DateTime

The DateTime object contains the basic mechanisms for managing dates and time.

Constructors

The following listing shows a simple example:

```
using System;

public class Demo
{
        public static void Main()
        {
```

```
DateTime x = new DateTime(
        1978,            // year
        9,               // month
        8,               // day
        18,              // hour
        35,              // minute
        5,               // second
        15);

Console.WriteLine("{0:F}", x);
    }
}
```

We call the constructor of the DateTime object and pass a set of parameters to it. The meaning of the various parameters is described by the comments on the right edge of the code. To display the content of the object, we call the WriteLine object. The result can be seen in the following line:

```
[hs@localhost mono]$ mono main.exe
Friday, 08 September 1978 18:35:05
```

The constructor has been overloaded several times, so you need not pass all parameters to it.

Comparing Dates

Whenever it's necessary to compare dates to one another, you can use the predefined methods provided by the Mono framework. In this section, we see how to compare dates with each other.

The easiest way to do the job is to use Compare. All you have to do is to pass parameters to the method and Mono does the rest for you. The next example shows how two dates can be retrieved from the command line. In addition, the two dates are compared to each other:

```
using System;

public class Demo
{
    public static void Main(string[] args)
    {
        DateTime x = DateTime.Parse(args[0]);
        DateTime y = DateTime.Parse(args[1]);

        Console.WriteLine("{0}", DateTime.Compare(x, y));
        Console.WriteLine("{0}", DateTime.Compare(x, x));
        Console.WriteLine("{0}", DateTime.Compare(y, x));
    }
}
```

Before we can compare data, we have to parse it. As you've already seen several times, the Parse method is the correct approach to use. In our example, we perform three comparisons so that you can see how Mono reacts. The output is displayed on the screen:

```
[hs@duron datum]$ mono datum.exe 'Friday, 08 September 1978 18:35:05'
'Friday, 08 September 1978 18:35:59'
-1
0
1
```

If the first value is lower than the second one, Mono will return -1. If both values are the same, the result will be 0. If the second value is lower than the first one, the output will be 1.

Leap Years

Leap years are essential and must be taken into consideration when working with time and date. Since 46 BC, a rule of thumb invented by Gaius Julius Caesar has existed. The rule says that if a year can be divided by four, it is a leap year. This works in most cases, but it isn't completely correct. With the introduction of the Gregorian calendar on February 24, 1582, the rule has changed slightly. According to this calendar, it is true that a year is a leap year when it can be divided by four. In addition, years that can be divided by 400 are leap years as well. However, years that can be divided by 100 but not by 400 are not leap years. This basic rule is still valid.

Because finding leap years is an uncomfortable thing, the Mono framework provides basic methods to do the job for you. In the following listing, you can see a simple program that analyzes a year:

```
using System;

public class Demo
{
        public static void Main(string[] args)
        {
                int year;

                foreach (string x in args)
                {
                        try
                        {
                                year = Int32.Parse(x);
                                Console.Write("{0}: ", year);
                                Console.WriteLine(
                                        DateTime.IsLeapYear(year));
                        }
                }
```

```
                    catch (Exception e)
                    {
                            Console.WriteLine("Error: {0}", x);
                    }
              }
        }
}
```

We parse the data that's sent to the program via the command line. After that, we call
DateTime.IsLeapYear. Depending on whether a year is a leap year or not, this method will
return true or false.

The next listing shows how our example can be used:

```
[hs@localhost mono]$ mono main.exe   1900 2000 2002 2004
1900: False
2000: True
2002: False
2004: True
```

Attributes and Static Methods

The DateTime object provides a rich set of attributes that make daily life with the software
much easier. In the next example, you learn to access those attributes:

```
using System;

public class Demo
{
        public static void Main(string[] args)
        {
                DateTime x = DateTime.Parse(args[0]);
                Console.WriteLine("String: {0}", x);
                Console.WriteLine("Date: {0}", x.Date);
                Console.WriteLine("Day: {0}", x.Day);
                Console.WriteLine("Day of the week: {0}", x.DayOfWeek);
                Console.WriteLine("Day of the year: {0}", x.DayOfYear);
                Console.WriteLine("Hour: {0}", x.Hour);
                Console.WriteLine("Microsecond: {0}", x.Millisecond);
                Console.WriteLine("Minute: {0}", x.Minute);
                Console.WriteLine("Month: {0}", x.Month);
                Console.WriteLine("Now: {0}", DateTime.Now);
                Console.WriteLine("Second: {0}", x.Second);
```

```
Console.WriteLine("Ticks: {0}", x.Ticks);
Console.WriteLine("Time of the day: {0}", x.TimeOfDay);
Console.WriteLine("Current date: {0}",
        DateTime.Today);
Console.WriteLine("Universal Time: {0}",
        DateTime.UtcNow);
Console.WriteLine("Year: {0}", x.Year);
    }
}
```

The listing contains all relevant attributes and static methods.

In the next listing, we compile the output of the program:

```
[hs@localhost mono]$ mono main.exe 'Friday, 08 September 1978 18:35:05'
String: Friday, 08 September 1978 18:35:05
Date: Friday, 08 September 1978 00:00:00
Day: 8
Day of the week: Friday
Day of the year: 251
Hour: 18
Microsecond: 0
Minute: 35
Month: 9
Now: Saturday, 03 May 2003 13:59:39
Second: 5
Ticks: 624097245050000000
Time of the day: 18:35:05
Current date: Saturday, 03 May 2003 00:00:00
Universal Time: Saturday, 03 May 2003 11:59:39
Year: 1978
```

TimeSpan

Until now, you've learned to work with fixed moments in time. Whenever it's necessary to work with intervals, you'll need a class called TimeSpan. In this section, we will deal with this class in detail.

Constructor
The constructor of the TimeSpan object has been overloaded several times. In the next example, you can see how an interval can be defined. We've included all constructors provided by Mono in the next piece of code:

```
using System;

public class Demo
{
        public static void Main(string[] args)
        {
                TimeSpan ts1 = new TimeSpan(Int32.MaxValue);
                Console.WriteLine("Value 1: {0}", ts1);

                TimeSpan ts2 = new TimeSpan(13, 32, 59);
                Console.WriteLine("Value 2: {0}", ts2);

                TimeSpan ts3 = new TimeSpan(13, 32, 59, 14);
                Console.WriteLine("Value 3: {0}", ts3);

                TimeSpan ts4 = new TimeSpan(13, 32, 59, 14, 54);
                Console.WriteLine("Value 4: {0}", ts4);
        }
}
```

The output of the program can be seen in the following listing:

```
[hs@localhost mono]$ mono main.exe
Value 1: 00:03:34.7483647
Value 2: 13:32:59
Value 3: 14.08:59:14
Value 4: 14.08:59:14.0540000
```

Depending on the constructor we take, Mono displays a different output.

Attributes

The TimeSpan class provides a rich set of attributes. We deal with those attributes in this section.

The next example shows how an instance can be created and how the attributes of that instance can be retrieved:

```
using System;

public class Demo
{
        public static void Main(string[] args)
        {
```

```
TimeSpan ts = new TimeSpan(13, 32, 59, 14, 54);

Console.WriteLine("Days: " + ts.Days);
Console.WriteLine("Hours: " + ts.Hours);
Console.WriteLine("Microseconds: " + ts.Milliseconds);
Console.WriteLine("Minutes: " + ts.Minutes);
Console.WriteLine("Seconds: " + ts.Seconds);
Console.WriteLine("Ticks: " + ts.Ticks);
Console.WriteLine("Total days: " + ts.TotalDays);
Console.WriteLine("Total hours: " + ts.TotalHours);
Console.WriteLine("Total microseconds: "
            + ts.TotalMilliseconds);
Console.WriteLine("Total minutes: " + ts.TotalMinutes);
Console.WriteLine("Total seconds: " + ts.TotalSeconds);
        }
}
```

In general, there are two types of attributes you can use. The first group contains the values we've passed to the constructor. The second group contains values that have been computed by Mono. The following listing describes what we want to express:

```
[hs@localhost mono]$ mono main.exe
Days: 14
Hours: 8
Microseconds: 54
Minutes: 59
Seconds: 14
Ticks: 12419540540000
Total days: 14.3744682175926
Total hours: 344.987237222222
Total microseconds: 1241954054
Total minutes: 20699.2342333333
Total seconds: 1241954.054
```

Simple Calculations

The TimeSpan class is essential for performing all kinds of mathematical operations. In this section, we take a look at the most fundamental operations:

```
using System;

public class Demo
{
        public static void Main(string[] args)
        {
```

```
TimeSpan ts1 = new TimeSpan(12, 12, 12, 32, 30);
TimeSpan ts2 = new TimeSpan(3, 9, 0, 2, 5);

Console.WriteLine("Sum: {0}", ts1 + ts2);
Console.WriteLine("      {0}", ts1.Add(ts2));

Console.WriteLine("Difference: {0}", ts1 - ts2);
Console.WriteLine("Comparison: {0}", ts1 < ts2 );
    }
}
```

In our example, we create two time spans. After that, we compute the sum of the two
instances we created. As you can see in the code, we've done this twice. First we used the +
operator. In addition to that, we called the static method Add. After computing the difference
of those two intervals, we perform a comparison:

```
[hs@localhost mono]$ mono main.exe
Sum: 15.21:12:34.0350000
     15.21:12:34.0350000
Difference: 9.03:12:30.0250000
Comparison: False
```

DateTime and TimeSpan

In many situations, DateTime and TimeSpan are used as a team. Here's an example:

```
using System;

public class Demo
{
    public static void Main(string[] args)
    {
        TimeSpan ts = new TimeSpan(13, 32, 59, 14, 54);
        DateTime dt =
            DateTime.Parse("04/05/2002 16:41:50");

        // Console.WriteLine("Sum 1: {0}", ts + dt);
        Console.WriteLine("Sum 2: {0}", dt + ts);
    }
}
```

In the preceding code, we try to add an instance of DateTime to an instance of TimeSpan. This
operation isn't possible because the desired operator is not available (we've marked the line

with //). The + operator is not defined for both operations. If you uncomment the first addition, the compiler will report an error. Luckily, this error occurs at compiler time and not at runtime, so it's fairly easy to find out that something has gone wrong. However, if you're working with dynamic type conversions, this could be a problem.

The next listing shows us the output we can expect:

```
[hs@localhost mono]$ mono main.exe
Sum 2: Saturday, 20 April 2002 01:41:04
```

The calculation is performed correctly. Working with TimeSpan and DateTime is essential, but we don't deal with further details because doing so would be far beyond the scope of this book.

In Brief

- Mono provides several classes for dealing with dates and time.

- All classes can deal with leap years.

- TimeSpan can be used to store intervals.

- DateTime represents a certain moment in time.

Database Programming

Databases are a fundamental component. Microsoft has tried several times to implement a database abstraction layer, but things have changed too often. It has become a real mess and it's hard to keep track of all these database interfaces such as ODBC, OLEDB, RDO, DAO, and ADO. Microsoft is currently in favor of ADO.NET, which is supposed to be the abstraction layer for all databases. Let's hope that Microsoft finally calms down and provides a consistent solution.

In this chapter, we focus entirely on database programming. You'll see how simple database applications can be built with Mono and how data can be retrieved from a database.

The Basic Concepts of ADO.NET

As mentioned in the introduction to this chapter, Microsoft is the world champion when it comes to redesigning and changing software. ADO.NET is currently the ultimate solution, so it's time to take a closer look at the basic concepts of this abstraction layer.

The architecture of ADO.NET is comparatively complex and can hardly be compared to a straightforward implementation, such as Perl's DBI layer. In this section, we try to explain the most important classes and make things a little bit clearer. As the Open Source counterpart of .NET, Mono tries to be 100%-compliant with Microsoft's specifications.

Figure 13.1 contains an overview of ADO.NET's architecture. As you can see, the architecture is quite complex yet flexible.

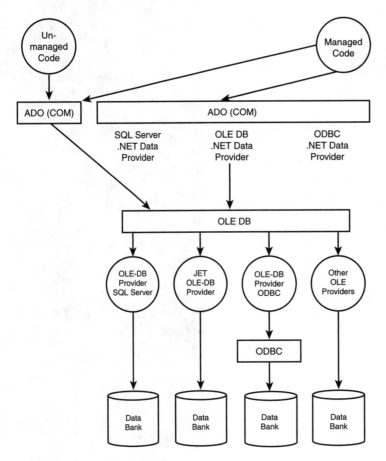

FIGURE 13.1   ADO.NET.

ADO.NET is just a part of a more complete concept. The System.Data contains some more objects that are essential for processing data. However, in this book we deal only with ADO.NET.

Let's get started and see how Mono's database interfaces work. Accessing a database can be done with the help of *.NET data providers*. .NET data providers are some sort of standard driver that tells Mono how a database can be accessed. The basic architecture can be compared with ODBC because ODBC provides a homogenous interface to many different data types as well.

Offline Access

When working with ADO.NET, it's important to know that the connection to the database is terminated as soon as the entire data has been read. This is essential and it influences the server-side transaction processing. In other words: Data is requested and processed on the client.

ADO.NET—The Details

ADO.NET is slightly different from ADO and it's hard to compare those two concepts. The RecordSet class does not exist anymore. Instead of RecordSet, you have to use DataSet, DataTable, and DataReader. The main advantage is that DataSet is capable of storing more than just one table and managing the connection between these tables. Inside the DataSet object, a table can be represented as an instance of System.Data.DataTable. For reading the data in the tables, Mono provides the DataReader class. It's important to mention that data is read sequentially—jumping around inside the result set is not supported. This is an important restriction. An additional restriction is that data can only be read exactly once. The reason for that is comparatively simple: Because there is no active connection to the database, this leads to an enormous performance boost.

All the Way to the Data

To access data in a database, some basic steps have to be made. First of all, an instance of OleDbConnection is established. All parameters of the connection are passed to this instance. In the next step, an instance of OleDbCommand is generated and the Connection attribute of OleDbConnection is bound. In addition, the actual SQL code is used as an attribute of OleDbCommand. To retrieve the data, a loop has to be executed.

The way to the data is hard and complex, but the entire process is on a high abstraction level, which can be an advantage.

Simple Interactions and the Installation Process

In this book, we use PostgreSQL to show you how you can work with databases. PostgreSQL, Firebird, and SAP DB are the three most sophisticated Open Source databases available. They provide numerous highly developed features that are essential for implementing professional applications. PostgreSQL is widely used by expert database developers and is already used in business-critical environments.

PostgreSQL is very close to the ANSI SQL standards and can be administered easily, so it's the perfect database for training and advanced applications.

Before we get back to Mono, let's take a brief look at the installation process of PostgreSQL.

Installing PostgreSQL

The source code of PostgreSQL can be downloaded freely from `ftp://ftp.de.postgresql.de/mirror/postgresql`. After downloading the code, the database can be installed with the help of a simple shell script:

```
#!/bin/sh

tar xvfz postgresql-7.3.tar.gz
cd postgresql-7.3
CFLAGS=' -O3 ' ./configure --prefix=/usr/local/postgresql-7.3
gmake
gmake install


mkdir /tmp/db
/usr/local/postgresql-7.3/bin/initdb -D /tmp/db
```

After installing the code, you can start the database instance:

```
[hs@duron src]$ /usr/local/postgresql-7.3/bin/pg_ctl -D /tmp/db/ -l
/dev/null -o "-i" start
postmaster successfully started
[hs@duron src]$ /usr/local/postgresql-7.3/bin/psql -l
      List of databases
   Name    ¦ Owner ¦ Encoding
-----------+-------+-----------
 template0 ¦ hs    ¦ SQL_ASCII
 template1 ¦ hs    ¦ SQL_ASCII
(2 rows)
```

`psql -l` lists all databases on the system. To create new databases, you can use `createdb`.

```
[hs@duron hs]$ createdb test
CREATE DATABASE
```

Database Connections

In this section, you learn to establish database connections. In contrast to other programming languages' respective frameworks, Mono does not provide a `Connect` function. Establishing a connection to the server is not done with one line, as you can see in the next listing:

```
using System;
using System.Data;
```

```
using Mono.Data.PostgreSqlClient;

class    Demo
{
        static void Main(string[] args)
        {
                try
                {
                        PgSqlConnection cnc = new PgSqlConnection ();
                        string connectionString =
                                "host=localhost;dbname=test;user=hs";
                        cnc.ConnectionString =  connectionString;
                        cnc.Open();
                        cnc.Close();
                }
                catch   (Exception e)
                {
                        Console.WriteLine("Fehler: " + e.Message);
                }
        }
}
```

After integrating all relevant modules, we create an instance of the PgSqlConnection object. This object contains a connection to the database. As you can see, we do not pass connection parameters to the constructor. The parameters of the connection we're going to establish are just attributes of the PgSqlConnection object. To define this variable, we assign a string to ConnectionString. After that, we can establish the connection to the database by calling Open. If an error occurs, we Catch it. Don't forget to use the correct user. In this example, we used a hardcoded connection string. If you get a No pg_hba.conf entry for host error, you have to reconfigure your database instance.

When compiling the program, we have to pass some flags to the compiler. That's necessary because otherwise Mono won't find the namespace we're looking for:

```
[hs@duron tmp]$ mcs pg.cs -r System.Data.dll -r
Mono.Data.PostgreSqlClient.dll
Compilation succeeded
[hs@duron tmp]$ mono pg.exe
```

Without mentioning the DLL, the code will not compile properly.

Creating Tables

The following example shows how tables can be created. All we need is the CREATE TABLE command. Keep in mind that this command won't return data, so we can send it to PostgreSQL with the help of ExecuteNonQuery:

```
class    Demo
{
        static void Main(string[] args)
        {
                try
                {
                        PgSqlConnection cnc = new PgSqlConnection ();
                        string connectionString =
                                "host=localhost;dbname=test;user=hs";
                        cnc.ConnectionString =  connectionString;
                        cnc.Open();

                        IDbCommand cmd = cnc.CreateCommand();
                        cmd.CommandText = "CREATE TABLE t_data "
                                + "(id serial, data text) ";
                        cmd.ExecuteNonQuery ();

                        cnc.Close();
                }
                catch    (Exception e)
                {
                        Console.WriteLine("Error: " + e.Message);
                }
        }
}
```

After we've established the connection to the database, we create a command. We'll execute this command later in the program. Again the entire block is inside a try/catch mechanism. When we execute the program, the listing will look like this:

```
[hs@duron tmp]$ mono pg.exe
NOTICE:  CREATE TABLE will create implicit sequence 't_data_id_seq' for
SERIAL column 't_data.id'
[hs@duron tmp]$ psql -c "\d" test
```

```
      List of relations
    Name     ¦   Type   ¦ Owner
---------------+----------+-------
 t_data       ¦ table    ¦ hs
 t_data_id_seq ¦ sequence ¦ hs
(2 rows)
```

As you can see, the table exists.

Inserting and Modifying Data

Data can easily be added to a table inside the database. In the case of PostgreSQL, there are two possibilities: You can use either INSERT or COPY. When importing a lot of data, COPY is about six times faster than INSERT (depending on your data structure, the amount of data, and so forth, of course). In this section, you learn about INSERT and UPDATE.

The following example shows how INSERT can be used:

```csharp
using System;
using System.Data;
using Mono.Data.PostgreSqlClient;

class   Demo
{
        static void Main(string[] args)
        {
                try
                {
                        PgSqlConnection cnc = new PgSqlConnection ();
                        string connectionString =
                                "host=localhost;dbname=test;user=hs";
                        cnc.ConnectionString =  connectionString;
                        cnc.Open();

                        IDbCommand cmd = cnc.CreateCommand();
                        cmd.CommandText = "CREATE TABLE t_data "
                                + "(id serial, data text) ";
                        cmd.ExecuteNonQuery ();

                        for     (int i = 0; i < 5; i++)
                        {
                                cmd.CommandText = "INSERT INTO "
                                        + "t_data (data) VALUES ('"
```

```
                                        + i + "')";
                        cmd.ExecuteNonQuery ();
                }

                cnc.Close();
        }
        catch   (Exception e)
        {
                Console.WriteLine("Error: " + e.Message);
        }
    }
}
```

In this example, we create a table containing five values. We do this with the help of simple INSERT statements. When starting the program, the data will be added instantly. If you get a PGRES_FATAL_ERROR ERROR: Relation 't_data_id_seq' already exists message, there is already a sequence called t_data_id_seq in the database. Just drop the sequence (DROP SEQUENCE t_data_id_seq) before executing the code. In the next listing, you can see which data we added to the table in our PostgreSQL database:

```
psql test

test=# SELECT * FROM t_data ;
 id ¦ data
----+------
  1 ¦ 0
  2 ¦ 1
  3 ¦ 2
  4 ¦ 3
  5 ¦ 4
(5 rows)
```

UPDATE statements work pretty similarly to INSERT, so you won't face too many problems. However, it's often necessary to find out how many rows a statement has changed:

```
using System;
using System.Data;
using Mono.Data.PostgreSqlClient;

class   Demo
{
        static void Main(string[] args)
        {
```

```
PgSqlConnection cnc = new PgSqlConnection ();
cnc.ConnectionString =  "host=localhost;"
        + "dbname=test;user=hs";
cnc.Open();

IDbCommand cmd = cnc.CreateCommand();
cmd.CommandText = "UPDATE t_data "
        + "SET data = 'updated' ";
int number = cmd.ExecuteNonQuery ();

if      (number == 0 )
{
        Console.WriteLine("no changes");
}
else if (number > 0)
{
        Console.WriteLine("changed: " + number);
}
else
{
        Console.WriteLine("error ...");
}

cnc.Close();
    }
}
```

We again use ExecuteNonQuery. This time the number of records affected by the UPDATE statement is returned as an integer value. The following listing shows the output we can expect from the program:

```
[hs@duron db]$ mono pg.exe
changed: 5
```

In this example, five records have been changed.

Simple Queries

Until now, we've added and modified data inside the database. In this section, we see how data can be selected. You'll find out that Mono provides simple methods for performing this job, so fetching data from the database isn't a problem at all.

The next code fragment focuses on simple SELECT statements. Let's have a look:

```
using System;
using System.Data;
using Mono.Data.PostgreSqlClient;

class   Demo
{
        static void Main(string[] args)
        {
                PgSqlConnection cnc = new PgSqlConnection ();
                cnc.ConnectionString =  "host=localhost;"
                        + "dbname=test;user=hs";
                cnc.Open();

                IDbCommand comm = cnc.CreateCommand ();
                comm.CommandType = CommandType.Text;
                comm.CommandText = "SELECT id, data FROM t_data ";

                IDataReader dr;
                dr = comm.ExecuteReader(CommandBehavior.SingleResult);

                for (int i = 0; i < 3; i++)
                {
                        dr.Read();
                        Console.WriteLine("Id: {0}, Text: {1}", dr[0], dr[1]);
                }

                cnc.Close();
        }
}
```

Again we open a connection to the database, and we define an SQL statement. In this scenario, we send a simple text to the database. We'll see later which other kinds of queries you can use. In the next step, we create an instance of IDataReader. To read the data, we use a simple loop. In our case, we want to read the first three records. To read exactly one line, we use the Read method. The fields of a record can be easily retrieved. All we have to do is to access the various elements.

The result is in no way surprising:

```
[hs@duron db]$ mono pg.exe
Id: 1, Text: updated
Id: 2, Text: updated
Id: 3, Text: updated
```

In the previous example, we haven't displayed the entire result. In most cases, this just isn't enough. When implementing practical examples, the query must be more flexible. For that purpose, it's necessary to define some parameters at runtime and not at compile time. The next example shows how information can be fetched at runtime:

```
using System;
using System.Data;
using Mono.Data.PostgreSqlClient;

class    Demo
{
        static void Main(string[] args)
        {
                int nRows = 0;
                int c = 0;
                string metadataValue, dataValue,  output;

                PgSqlConnection cnc = new PgSqlConnection ();
                cnc.ConnectionString =  "host=localhost;"
                        + "dbname=test;user=hs";
                cnc.Open();

                // the first parameter is the SQL statement
                IDbCommand comm = cnc.CreateCommand ();
                comm.CommandType = CommandType.Text;
                comm.CommandText = args[0];

                IDataReader rdr;
                rdr = comm.ExecuteReader(CommandBehavior.SingleResult);
                DataTable dt = rdr.GetSchemaTable();

                // processing the data
                while    ( rdr.Read() )
                {
                        Console.WriteLine("Row " + nRows + ": ");
                        for     (c = 0; c < rdr.FieldCount; c++)
                        {
                                DataRow dr = dt.Rows[c];
                                metadataValue = " Column " + c + ": "
                                        + dr["ColumnName"];

                                if      ( rdr.IsDBNull(c) == true )
                                {
```

```
                                    dataValue = " is NULL";
                        }
                        else
                        {
                                    dataValue = ": " + rdr.GetValue(c);
                        }

                        output = metadataValue + dataValue;
                        Console.WriteLine(output);
                }
                nRows++;
        }

        cnc.Close();
    }
}
```

We process the data line by line. For every column, we extract its name and the corresponding value. Extracting data can easily be done with the help of `GetValue`. To find out whether a certain cell contains a NULL value, you can call the `IsDBNull` method. In addition, it's important to find out which data structure the SQL statement has returned. For that purpose, we use the `GetSchemaTable` method.

Let's look at the output:

```
[hs@duron db]$ mono pg.exe "SELECT * FROM t_data"
Row 0:
  Column 0: id: 1
  Column 1: data: updated
Row 1:
  Column 0: id: 2
  Column 1: data: updated
Row 2:
  Column 0: id: 3
  Column 1: data: updated
Row 3:
  Column 0: id: 4
  Column 1: data: updated
Row 4:
  Column 0: id: 5
  Column 1: data: updated
```

As we have already seen, the table contains exactly five records.

Exception Handling

Exception handling is important in more cases than just when working with databases. In this section, you learn about the most basic concepts of exception handling. The next piece of code shows how a simple error can be caught:

```
using System;
using System.Data;
using Mono.Data.PostgreSqlClient;

class    Demo
{
        static void Main(string[] args)
        {
                try
                {
                        PgSqlConnection cnc = new PgSqlConnection ();
                        cnc.ConnectionString =  "host=localhost;"
                                + "dbname=test-xxx;user=hs";
                        cnc.Open();
                        cnc.Close();
                }
                catch   (PgSqlException e)
                {
                        Console.WriteLine("Error: " + e);

                }
        }
}
```

PgSqlException is the relevant object. The following listing contains a typical error:

```
[hs@duron db]$ mono pg.exe
Error: PgSqlError:FATAL:  Database "test-xxx" does not exist in the
system catalog.
: Could not connect to database. <Stack Trace>
```

Metadata

This section deals briefly with metadata. *Metadata* is information that can be extracted from the result. The number of rows and the number of columns in a result set are good examples.

However, there's also some additional information available that can be useful. In the next example, we read the entire set of metadata provided by Mono and PostgreSQL:

```
using System;
using System.Data;
using Mono.Data.PostgreSqlClient;

class    Demo
{
        static void Main(string[] args)
        {
                PgSqlConnection cnc = new PgSqlConnection ();
                cnc.ConnectionString =  "host=localhost;"
                        + "dbname=test;user=hs";
                cnc.Open();

                IDbCommand comm = cnc.CreateCommand ();
                comm.CommandType = CommandType.Text;
                comm.CommandText = "SELECT id, data FROM t_data ";

                IDataReader dr;
                dr = comm.ExecuteReader(CommandBehavior.SingleResult);
                DataTable dt = dr.GetSchemaTable();

                Console.WriteLine("Columns: " + dt.Rows.Count);

                // processing metadata
                foreach (DataRow one in dt.Rows)
                {
                        foreach (DataColumn two in dt.Columns)
                        {
                                Console.WriteLine(two.ColumnName
                                        +  " = " + one[two]);
                        }
                        Console.WriteLine("\n");
                }

                cnc.Close();
        }
}
```

Again we use `GetSchemaTable` to extract the data structure from the result set. After that, we enter a `foreach` loop that displays some useful information:

```
[hs@duron db]$ mono pg.exe
Columns: 2
ColumnName = id
ColumnOrdinal = 1
ColumnSize = 4
NumericPrecision = 0
NumericScale = 0
IsUnique = False
IsKey =
BaseCatalogName =
BaseColumnName = id
BaseSchemaName =
BaseTableName =
DataType = System.Int32
AllowDBNull = False
ProviderType = 23
IsAliased = False
IsExpression = False
IsIdentity = False
IsAutoIncrement = False
IsRowVersion = False
IsHidden = False
IsLong = False
IsReadOnly = False


ColumnName = data
ColumnOrdinal = 2
ColumnSize = -1
NumericPrecision = 0
NumericScale = 0
IsUnique = False
IsKey =
BaseCatalogName =
BaseColumnName = data
BaseSchemaName =
BaseTableName =
DataType = System.String
AllowDBNull = False
ProviderType = 25
```

```
IsAliased = False
IsExpression = False
IsIdentity = False
IsAutoIncrement = False
IsRowVersion = False
IsHidden = False
IsLong = False
IsReadOnly = False
```

Most of the information is retrieved from PostgreSQL's internal system tables and passed to Mono. This process is hidden from the user, so you need not worry about it too much.

Transactions

Transactions are an essential component of modern database technology. The code for managing transactions inside the Mono framework is currently still beta, so it's still necessary to be careful when using this feature in combination with Mono.

Cursors

Most advanced modern database systems provide what are known as *cursors*. The main advantage of cursors is that the result is returned to the client as one recordset. Whenever the next value in a cursor is requested, the database computes it in real time and returns it to the client. In other words: The result of a query is generated and returned line by line. The client has to store exactly one line of data. Whenever it's necessary to process gigabytes of data, cursors are essential because otherwise it will be hard to keep the entire recordset in memory.

In the next example, you can see how cursors work. We use the interactive command shell (psql) to see what you have to do:

```
mono=# DECLARE mycurs CURSOR FOR SELECT 1+1 UNION SELECT 2+2;
DECLARE CURSOR
mono=# FETCH mycurs;
 ?column?
----------
        2
(1 row)

mono=# FETCH mycurs;
```

```
 ?column?
-----------
         4
(1 row)

mono=# FETCH mycurs;
 ?column?
-----------
(0 rows)

mono=# COMMIT;
COMMIT
```

Most drivers for the Mono framework currently don't support cursors, but there are already serious efforts being made to implement cursors. If it isn't possible to work without cursors, you need not resign because you can use external C libraries to do the job for you. In this section, we won't deal with cursors in great detail.

Writing Simple Stored Procedures

In this section, we examine stored procedures. Mono provides some simple and easy-to-use methods for working with stored procedures. We'll take a closer look at these features later in this section.

An example for server-side functions is version(). It returns the current version of PostgreSQL and some additional information about the compiler and the operating system:

```
mono=# SELECT version();
                                version
----------------------------------------------------------------------
 PostgreSQL 7.3.2 on i686-pc-linux-gnu, compiled by GCC gcc (GCC) 3.2
 20020903 (Red Hat Linux 8.0 3.2-7)
(1 row)
```

When using Mono's database abstraction layer to perform this query, we can write a program as shown in the next example:

```
using System;
using System.Data;
using Mono.Data.PostgreSqlClient;

class    Demo
{
        static void Main(string[] args)
```

```
        {
                PgSqlConnection cnc = new PgSqlConnection ();
                cnc.ConnectionString =  "host=localhost;"
                        + "dbname=test;user=hs";
                cnc.Open();

                IDbCommand callStoredProcCommand = cnc.CreateCommand ();
                object data;

                callStoredProcCommand.CommandType =
                        CommandType.StoredProcedure;
                callStoredProcCommand.CommandText = "version";
                data = callStoredProcCommand.ExecuteScalar ();

                Console.WriteLine("Version: " + data );

                cnc.Close();
        }
}
```

After establishing a connection to the database, we create an instance of the IDbCommand
object. We tell the instance that we want to call a stored procedure (CommandType.
StoredProcedure). In the next step, we assign the name of the procedure to the object.
Internally, the driver compiles an SQL statement that can be executed. Finally, we read the
result of the query. Just as always, we use Console.WriteLine to display the result.

The output is shown in the next listing:

```
[hs@duron db]$ mono pg.exe
Version: PostgreSQL 7.3.2 on i686-pc-linux-gnu, compiled by GCC gcc (GCC)
3.2 20020903 (Red Hat Linux 8.0 3.2-7)
```

Stored Procedures and Function Overloading

When talking about server-side functions, it's necessary to think about function overloading—at least in the case of PostgreSQL. Server-side function overloading is no different from
client-side function overloading.

Let's try to implement an additional function called version. This time it accepts an integer
variable as an input parameter. Before we can implement the function, we'll add PL/pgSQL to
the database called test:

```
[hs@duron tmp]$ createlang plpgsql test
NOTICE:  CreateProceduralLanguage: changing return type of function
plpgsql_call_handler() from OPAQUE to LANGUAGE_HANDLER
```

Now we can implement the desired version of the function:

```
CREATE OR REPLACE FUNCTION version(int) RETURNS text AS '
        BEGIN
                RETURN $1::text;
        END;
' LANGUAGE 'plpgsql';

CREATE OR REPLACE FUNCTION version(int, int) RETURNS text AS '
        BEGIN
                RETURN ($1 + $2)::text;
        END;
' LANGUAGE 'plpgsql';

SELECT version();
SELECT version(3);
SELECT version(4, 3);
```

In the following listing, you can see how the new functions could be added to the database and how different versions of version can be called:

```
[hs@duron tmp]$ psql test < function.sql
CREATE FUNCTION
CREATE FUNCTION
                                version
----------------------------------------------------------------
 PostgreSQL 7.3.2 on i686-pc-linux-gnu, compiled by GCC gcc (GCC) 3.2
 20020903 (Red Hat Linux 8.0 3.2-7)
(1 row)

 version
---------
 3
(1 row)

 version
---------
 7
(1 row)
```

The problem now is that we have to find out which method Mono should call.

Functions accepting many different parameter sets can currently be used only in combination with strings, which is a significant restriction. In addition, older versions of Mono do not support the public PgSqlParameter(string *parameterName*, DbType *dbType*) constructor.

Additional Features

All database modules are currently still under heavy development, so you can expect that many database drivers will provide many new features in the future.

If you need additional information about Mono and databases, check out www.go-mono.org. There you'll find additional hints about databases and database drivers.

In Brief

- Mono provides a powerful interface to all commonly used databases.

- Mono provides a database abstraction layer, named ADO.NET, which contains a rich set of functions for interacting with a database.

- Mono provides separate classes for catching exceptions thrown by the database.

- IDataReader provides methods to extract the schema of a result.

- With the help of metadata, you can find out about the result provided by the database.

- ADO.NET provides methods for interacting with stored procedures.

- Accessing overloaded server side functions is hard to do.

Mono and XML

In .NET, Microsoft has implemented a set of classes for working with XML and interfaces to it. Many common standards such as DOM, XPath, XSD, and XSLT are supported. Mono tries to support those standards as well and tries to implement Microsoft's classes as proposed by the .NET Framework. In addition, many classes have already been developed, so working with XML and Mono shouldn't cause too many problems.

The following list contains an overview of the most important standards supported by Mono and .NET:

- XML 1.0 (http://www.w3.org/TR/1998/REC-xml-19980210)

- XML namespaces (http://www.w3.org/TR/REC-xml-names)

- XSD Schemas (http://www.w3.org/2001/XMLSchema)

- XPath (http://www.w3.org/TR/xpath)

- XSLT (http://www.w3.org/TR/xslt)

- DOM Level 1 (http://www.w3.org/TR/REC-DOM-Level-1)

- DOM Level 2 (http://www.w3.org/TR/DOM-Level-2)

All together, five namespace for working with XML are provided:

- System.Xml

- System.Xml.Schema

- System.Xml.Serialization

- System.Xml.XPath

- System.Xml.Xsl

In this chapter, we deal with Mono extensively. You'll see many practical examples so that you can learn how Mono's interfaces to XML can be used efficiently.

Writing Simple Documents

The System.Xml namespace will help you to generate simple XML documents. Many programming languages provide nothing more than basic support for XML, which can make your daily work painful. System.Xml makes many situations much easier because it provides highly sophisticated classes. Many useful features are provided and it's easy to make use of them:

```
using System;
using System.Xml;

public class Demo
{
        public static void Main(string[] args)
        {
                XmlTextWriter wr =
                        new XmlTextWriter("/tmp/mono.xml", null);

                wr.Formatting = Formatting.Indented;
                wr.Indentation = 3;
                wr.WriteStartDocument();
                wr.Flush();
                wr.Close();
        }
}
```

First of all, we create an instance of XmlTextWriter. All we have to do is to pass the name of the file we want to create to the constructor. In the next step, we define some formats and start the document. Finally, we flush the buffer and quit the file. When we execute the program, a simple file will be created:

```
[hs@duron xml]$ cat /tmp/mono.xml
<?xml version="1.0"?>[hs@duron xml]$
```

Older versions of Mono provide the output you can see in the listing. Newer versions of Mono create an empty file.

As you can see, the example is easy. Now that you've seen how the most basic example can be created, it's time to have a look at how data can be added to the file:

```
using System;
using System.Xml;

public class Demo
{
        public static void Main(string[] args)
        {
                XmlTextWriter wr =
                        new XmlTextWriter("/tmp/mono.xml", null);

                wr.Formatting = Formatting.Indented;
                wr.Indentation = 3;
                wr.WriteStartDocument();

                wr.WriteComment("I am a comment");
                wr.WriteStartElement("data");

                wr.WriteElementString("product", "Bread");
                wr.WriteElementString("product", "Hot Dog");
                wr.WriteElementString("product", "<product></product>");

                wr.WriteEndElement();

                wr.Flush();
                wr.Close();
        }
}
```

Just as in the first example, we define the layout of the document. After that, we add a comment to the XML file. The text of the comment can be passed to the `WriteComment` method as a string. To add elements to the string, we call the `WriteElementString` method. The first parameter defines the tag. The second parameter contains the value we want to add. The first two records contain normal data, which means that there are no special symbols around. However, in the third record, we want store some critical data. At the end of the program, we terminate the file.

In the following listing, you can see the file Mono has created:

```
[hs@localhost mono]$ cat /tmp/mono.xml
<?xml version="1.0"?><!--I am a comment-->
<data>
   <product>Bread</product>
   <product>Hot Dog</product>
   <product>&lt;product&gt;&lt;/product&gt;</product>
```

The file doesn't contain any surprises. Still, the third record is important: Mono has escaped all symbols. That's an important fact because otherwise writing special characters to XML files would be critical.

Nested data is important when working with XML. If an element should contain many other elements, you can do that easily. All you have to do is to call WriteStartElement twice:

```
wr.WriteStartElement("data");
wr.WriteStartElement("data");

// some more code ...

wr.WriteEndElement();
wr.WriteEndElement();
```

The XML code will look like this:

```
<data>
    <data>

real data ...

    </data>
</data>
```

As you can see, creating hierarchical structures is an easy task.

Attributes and XmlTextWriter

The XmlTextWriter class contains some basic attributes. In this section, we take a closer look at those variables. Examine the code in the following listing:

```
using System;
using System.Xml;

public class Demo
{
        public static void Main(string[] args)
        {
                XmlTextWriter wr =
                        new XmlTextWriter("/tmp/mono.xml", null);
                wr.WriteStartDocument();
                wr.WriteStartElement("data");
                wr.WriteElementString("product", "Sausage");
                wr.WriteEndElement();
```

```
            Console.WriteLine("BaseStream: " + wr.BaseStream );
            Console.WriteLine("Formatting: " + wr.Formatting );
            Console.WriteLine("Indentation: " + wr.Indentation );
            Console.WriteLine("IndentChar: " + wr.IndentChar );
            Console.WriteLine("Namespaces: " + wr.Namespaces );
            Console.WriteLine("QuoteChar: " + wr.QuoteChar );
            Console.WriteLine("WriteState: " + wr.WriteState );
            Console.WriteLine("XmlLang: " + wr.XmlLang );
            Console.WriteLine("XmlSpace: " + wr.XmlSpace );

            wr.Flush();
            wr.Close();
        }
}
```

In this listing, we read all attributes and display the content of these variables on the screen. Let's have a closer look at the data we're going to extract:

- BaseStream: Contains the stream that will be used

- Formatting: Tells the system how the document should be formatted

- IndentChar: Defines an indent character

- Namespaces: Tells Mono whether namespaces should be used

- QuoteChar: Tells the systems which characters Mono should use to quote attributes

- WriteState: Returns the status of the writer

- XmlLang: Returns the scope of xml:lang

- XmlSpace: Returns xml:space

In the following listing, you'll see which information we can retrieve:

```
[hs@localhost mono]$ mono main.exe
BaseStream: System.IO.FileStream
Formatting: None
Indentation: 2
IndentChar:
Namespaces: True
QuoteChar: "
WriteState: Content
XmlLang:
XmlSpace: None
```

Type Conversions

It can be necessary to cast variables when creating an XML file. Therefore, Mono provides the XmlConvert class. In the next example, you can see how an integer value can be cast to a string:

```
using System;
using System.Xml;

public class Demo
{
        public static void Main(string[] args)
        {
                int x = 3;

                XmlTextWriter wr =
                        new XmlTextWriter("/tmp/mono.xml", null);
                wr.WriteStartDocument();
                wr.WriteElementString("data", XmlConvert.ToString(x));

                wr.Flush();
                wr.Close();
        }
}
```

ToString helps us to convert the integer value to a string. The content of /tmp/mono.xml is not surprising:

```
[hs@localhost mono]$ cat /tmp/mono.xml
<?xml version="1.0"?><data>3</data>
```

XmlConvert provides many additional methods that make type conversions truly simple. A complete list of all methods can be found in Microsoft's MSDN documentation.

Direct Writes

It's sometimes necessary to write data without using high-level functions. The next listing compiles an example to show us how things work:

```
using System;
using System.Xml;

public class Demo
{
```

```
public static void Main(string[] args)
{
        XmlTextWriter wr =
                new XmlTextWriter("/tmp/mono.xml", null);
        wr.WriteStartDocument();
        wr.WriteRaw("\n<data>\n" +
                "    <title>Mono</title>\n" +
                "</data>\n");
        wr.Flush();
        wr.Close();
}
}
```

This time we use WriteRaw to access the XML file directly. Keep in mind that it could easily happen that the XML file becomes invalid because there is no protection from Mono anymore. Therefore, we do not recommend using these functions unless you know perfectly well what you're doing.

When executing the program, four lines of XML code will be generated:

```
<?xml version="1.0"?>
<data>
    <title>Mono</title>
</data>
```

Reading XML Files

For reading data in an XML file, Mono provides a class called XmlReader. Reading an XML file is slightly more complex than writing one. In this section, we see how XML files can be read. Let's get started and have a look at an example:

```
using System;
using System.Xml;

public class Demo
{
        public static void Main(string[] args)
        {
                XmlTextReader r = new XmlTextReader("/tmp/mono.xml");
                string element;

                while  (r.Read())
                {
```

```
                    element = r.Name;
                    Console.WriteLine("Element: " + element);
            }
      }
}
```

At the beginning of the program, we create an instance of XmlTextReader. The name of the XML file is passed to the constructor. We use a loop to process the XML file. Inside the loop, we process every element. The result will look like this:

```
[hs@localhost mono]$ mono main.exe
Element: xml
Element:
Element: data
Element:
Element: title
Element:
Element: title
Element:
Element: data
```

In this example, you see which elements you can find inside the file. If you want to know which values are assigned to which fields, we need an additional method:

```
using System;
using System.Xml;

public class Demo
{
        public static void Main(string[] args)
        {
                XmlTextReader r = new XmlTextReader("/tmp/mono.xml");
                string element, data;

                while   (r.Read())
                {
                        Console.WriteLine(r.ReadString());
                }
        }
}
```

Unfortunately, ReadString has not been implemented yet. This is a real problem because implementing advanced applications is not possible—at least not if they support XML.

Mono will report an error (this will be fixed in future versions of Mono):

```
[hs@localhost mono]$ mono main.exe

Unhandled Exception: System.NotImplementedException: The requested
feature is not yet implemented
in <0x0002f> 00 System.Xml.XmlTextReader:ReadString ()
in <0x00057> 00 .Demo:Main (string[])
```

Mono isn't ready, so some features just haven't been implemented. The Mono framework is still under heavy development, so it will take some time until all features are implemented.

In Brief

- Mono provides a set of classes for interacting with an XML file.

- Support for XML has been constantly improved in more recent versions of Mono.

- With the help of XmlConvert, you can perform simple conversions.

- To create an XML file, you can write to the file directly or you can use make use of Mono's onboard functionality.

- The XmlTextReader object helps you read data from an XML file.

User Interfaces

Some years ago, text-based applications were the state of the art. Nowadays, things have changed significantly and the user can decide which desktop he wants to use. Desktops are built on graphical libraries such as GTK, Qt, and Xforms.

In this chapter, we focus entirely on implementing user interfaces. You'll see how Mono can be used in combination with graphical libraries. Currently, two modules are provided which will help you to implement wonderful user interfaces: GTK# and Qt#. Meanwhile, serious efforts are also made to provide Windows-compliant forms. At the moment, this isn't possible because there are still some major technical challenges that have to be solved The .NET user interface library is called `System.Windows.Forms`. It is hard to implement on non-Windows platforms because it exposes the internal Windows system calls, and also because many developers extend the library with widgets coded as Windows binaries.

This chapter is supposed to be an overview about user interfaces and Mono in general. Providing a reference would not make too much sense here because GTK# and Qt# are still under heavy development.

GTK#

The GTK libraries are the fundamental component of the popular GNOME desktop that's widely used on Unix platforms. According to many developers, standard tools just aren't suitable for implementing complex applications. Therefore, many people develop efficient tools so that you can implement user interfaces easily. GTK is an interesting platform for developing software because it's freely available under the terms of the GPL license.

In this section, we take a closer look at GTK# and you'll see which features the GTK# framework provides.

Installation

Let's have a look at the installation of GTK#. To download the sources, check out `http://gtk-sharp.sourceforge.net`. This section is based on GTK# 0.5.

After downloading the TAR archive, you can unpack the sources. To compile the code, you can use `configure` and `make`. When compiling samples, some errors can occur because some assemblies might not be found. In a situation like that, you can modify the makefile so that the samples won't be compiled anymore.

To make sure that Mono finds all libraries, the environment variables `MONO_PATH` and `LD_LIBRARY_PATH` must be set. After compiling and installing the code with the help of `configure`, `make`, and `make install`, GTK# can be used safely.

Simple Windows

In this section, you learn how simple windows can be drawn.

Windows and Buttons

Let's start with a simple example:

```
using Gtk;
using GtkSharp;
using System;
using System.Drawing;

public class MyButton
{
        public static void Main (string[] args)
        {
                Application.Init ();
                Window win = new Window ("My first button");
                win.DefaultSize = new Size (200, 200);
                Button btn = new Button ("Click");
                win.Add (btn);
                win.ShowAll ();
                Application.Run ();
        }
}
```

The application is truly simple. At the beginning of the program, we create a window and assign a name to it. After that, we define the size of the window and assign it to the window. In the next step, we define a button and assign text to it. The button is put into the window and displayed.

To compile the application, we need some special compiler flags:

```
[hs@duron mono]$ mcs main.cs /r:gtk-sharp /r:System.Drawing
Compilation succeeded
```

Don't forget to set LD_LIBRARY_PATH and MONO_PATH before compiling the code. It's important to link the program to the GTK libraries.

After compiling the code, we can start the program with the help of mint and mono. mint isn't really intended for end users. It is mush slower because it is an interpreted language, but it can sometimes help you to execute Mono binaries.

In the next step, we try to assign an event to the button. In this example, we want text to be displayed when the button is clicked. In addition, we want the window to be closed properly. The code of our application looks like this:

```
using Gtk;
using GtkSharp;
using System;
using System.Drawing;

public class MyButton
{
        public static void Main (string[] args)
        {
                Application.Init ();
                Window win = new Window ("My first button");
                win.DefaultSize = new Size (200, 200);
                win.DeleteEvent += new DeleteEventHandler (Fenster_Weg);
                Button btn = new Button ("Click");
                btn.Clicked += new EventHandler (button_press);
                win.Add (btn);
                win.ShowAll ();
                Application.Run ();
        }

        static void button_press (object obj, EventArgs args)
        {
                Console.WriteLine ("Button pressed");
        }
```

```
static void Fenster_Weg (object obj, DeleteEventArgs args)
{
        Application.Quit ();
        args.RetVal = true;
}
}
```

We must define an event handler that tells Mono which method should be called when. In our example, we define two event handlers: DeleteEventHandler is called when a window is closed, and EventHandler is called when somebody clicks the button. All methods started by an event handler must be static because they aren't called for an instance but for an event. We use an object and some parameters as input parameters.

After starting the program, a simple window is displayed as shown in Figure 15.1.

Scrollable Windows
GTK# supports scrollable windows. Whenever you have to display a lot of information that doesn't fit on one page, it's necessary to have a mechanism for scrolling. For generating a window like that, we have to use the ScrolledWindow object. However, we don't want to go into detail at this point.

FIGURE 15.1   A simple window.

Events
GTK# and X11 provide a rich set of events that you can use to implement high-level and wonderful-looking applications. The following list is an overview of all commonly used events:

- event

- button_press_event

- button_release_event

- motion_notify_event

- delete_event

- destroy_event

- expose_event

- key_press_event

- `key_release_event`

- `enter_notify_event`

- `leave_notify_event`

- `focus_in_event`

- `focus_out_event`

- `map_event`

- `unmap_event`

- `property_notify_event`

- `selection_clear_event`

- `selection_request_event`

- `selection_notify_event`

- `proximity_in_event`

- `proximity_out_event`

- `drag_begin_event`

- `drag_request_event`

- `drag_end_event`

- `drop_enter_event`

- `drop_leave_event`

- `drop_data_available_event`

- `other_event`

FIGURE 15.2   Important information.

Pictures

GTK# provides easy-to-use methods for displaying almost every kind of images. The Image object provides all relevant features, making it an essential component of GTK#. Let's look at the example in Figure 15.2.

Windows Containing Many Elements

Until now, you've seen how exactly one element can be added to a window. In this section, we get into more detail and see how multiple elements can be combined.

HBox and VBox

To add multiple elements to a window, we have to use an object called VBox. A VBox is nothing more than a simple vertical rectangle. If you want to create a horizontal rectangle, you use HBox. Let's have a look at some code so that you can see how things work:

```
using System;
using System.Drawing;
using Gtk;
using GtkSharp;

public class Demo
{
        public static void Main (string[] args)
        {
                Application.Init();
                Window win = new Window ("MyWindow");
                win.DeleteEvent += new DeleteEventHandler (Remove_Window);

                VBox box = new VBox (false, 2);

                Gtk.Image image1 = new Gtk.Image("/home/hs/logo_ext.jpg");
                box.PackStart(image1, true, true, 0);

                Gtk.Image image2 = new Gtk.Image("/home/hs/logo.jpg");
                box.PackStart(image2, true, true, 0);

                Gtk.Image image3 = new Gtk.Image("/home/hs/logo_ext.jpg");
                box.PackStart(image3, true, true, 0);

                win.Add (box);

                win.ShowAll ();
                Application.Run ();
        }

        static void Remove_Window (object o, DeleteEventArgs args)
        {
                Application.Quit();
        }
}
```

FIGURE 15.3 Multiple images.

We again create a window and then define an event so that the window can be closed easily. In the previous example, we didn't define events so that you could see what happens in situations with no events (don't forget to change the paths in the code).

After we create the box, we add three pictures to it. At the end of the program, we make sure that the entire box is added to the window. Mono displays a nice-looking window full of pictures, as demonstrated in Figure 15.3.

Defining Borders

The application you just saw does not look too professional because the images we added to the scenery seem to stick to the edge of the window—this definitely isn't beautiful.

In the next example, we want the images to be displayed near the edge of the window:

```csharp
using System;
using System.Drawing;
using Gtk;
using GtkSharp;

public class Demo
{
        public static void Main (string[] args)
        {
                Application.Init();
                Window win = new Window ("Main window");
                win.DeleteEvent += new DeleteEventHandler (Delete_Window);

                win.BorderWidth = 20;
                Gtk.Image image1 = new Gtk.Image("/home/hs/logo_ext.jpg");
                win.Add (image1);

                win.ShowAll ();
                Application.Run ();
        }

        static void Delete_Window (object o, DeleteEventArgs args)
        {
                Application.Quit();
        }
}
```

FIGURE 15.4   Nice-looking image.

We tell Mono that the distance between the picture and the edges of the windows should be 20 pixels. Figure 15.4 shows the improvement.

Frames and Labels

GTK# also provides frames and labels. With the help of those two elements, it's easy to create blocks and text. Assume that we're developing an application in which text should be added to a picture:

```
using System;
using System.Drawing;
using Gtk;
using GtkSharp;

public class Demo
{
        public static void Main (string[] args)
        {
                Application.Init();
                Window win = new Window ("Main window");
                win.DeleteEvent += new DeleteEventHandler (Remove_Window);

                VBox box = new VBox(false, 2);

                Frame frame = new Frame ("A cool frame");
                Label label = new Label ("A cool label");

                frame.Add (label);
                box.PackStart (frame, false, false, 0);

                win.BorderWidth = 20;
                Gtk.Image image1 = new Gtk.Image("/home/hs/logo_ext.jpg");

                box.Add(image1);
                win.Add(box);

                win.ShowAll ();
                Application.Run ();
        }
```

```
static void Remove_Window (object o, DeleteEventArgs args)
{
        Application.Quit();
}
}
```

We define a box to which the text and the corresponding label are added. In addition, we define a border around the objects. As you can see, Add is called many times. The output of the program can be seen in Figure 15.5.

We could have added the picture to the frame. In that case, the code would look like this:

FIGURE 15.5 Text and labels.

```
using System;
using System.Drawing;
using Gtk;
using GtkSharp;

public class Demo
{
        public static void Main (string[] args)
        {
                Application.Init();
                Window win = new Window ("Main window");
                win.DeleteEvent += new DeleteEventHandler (Remove_Window);
                win.BorderWidth = 20;

                VBox box = new VBox(false, 2);

                Frame frame1 = new Frame ("Frame 1");
                Label label1 = new Label ("Label 1");

                frame1.Add (label1);
                box.PackStart (frame1, false, false, 0);

                Frame frame2 = new Frame ("Frame 2");
                Gtk.Image image1 = new Gtk.Image("/home/hs/logo_ext.jpg");
```

```
        frame2.Add(image1);
        box.Add(frame2);
        win.Add(box);

        win.ShowAll ();
        Application.Run ();
    }

    static void Remove_Window (object o, DeleteEventArgs args)
    {
        Application.Quit();
    }
}
```

FIGURE 15.6   Text and labels again.

You won't see a huge difference in Figure 15.6, but the most important thing is that you can see and understand how labels, text, and images can be used in combination with C#.

Tables

Tables are a central feature of GTK#. With the help of tables, it's easy to arrange elements. In this example, we want to arrange a single button:

```
using System;
using System.Drawing;
using Gtk;
using GtkSharp;

public class Demo
{
        public static void Main (string[] args)
        {
                Application.Init();
                Window win = new Window ("Main window");
                win.DeleteEvent += new DeleteEventHandler (Remove_Window);
                win.BorderWidth = 20;
```

```
Button button1 = new Button("Button 1");
Button button2 = new Button("Button 2");

Table table = new Table(3, 3, true);

button1.Show();
button2.Show();

table.Attach(button1, 0, 2, 0, 1);
table.Attach(button2, 1, 3, 2, 3);

win.Add(table);

win.ShowAll ();
Application.Run ();
}

static void Remove_Window (object o, DeleteEventArgs args)
{
        Application.Quit();
}
}
```

After defining two buttons, we create a table of a certain size. The various elements are put into the appropriate fields, respectively; they're put into an area that contains many fields. Elements can be added with the help of the Attach method. At the end of the program, we add the table to the window (see Figure 15.7).

FIGURE 15.7 Two buttons added to a table.

Menus

Menus are important in modern desktop applications. Therefore, GTK# provides simple mechanisms for implementing comfortable, menu-driven user interfaces. In this section, we take a closer look at menus. Let's start with a simple example:

```
using System;
using System.Drawing;
using Gtk;
using GtkSharp;

public class Demo
{
        public static void Main (string[] args)
        {
```

```
            Application.Init();
            Window win = new Window("A Window ... :) ");
            win.DeleteEvent += new DeleteEventHandler(End_Delete);
            win.DefaultSize = new Size(200, 150);

            VBox box = new VBox (false, 2);

            // Creating MenuBar
            MenuBar mb = new MenuBar();
            Menu file_menu = new Menu();

            // Adding items
            MenuItem open_item = new MenuItem("Open");
            file_menu.Append(open_item);

            // Add an entry
            MenuItem exit_item = new MenuItem("Quit");
            exit_item.Activated += new EventHandler(Quit);
            file_menu.Append(exit_item);

            // The parent node
            MenuItem file_item = new MenuItem("File");
            file_item.Submenu = file_menu;
            mb.Append(file_item);
            box.PackStart(mb, false, false, 0);

            // Creating a button
            Button btn = new Button("Quit");
            btn.Clicked += new EventHandler(Quit);
            box.PackStart(btn, true, true, 0);

            win.Add (box);
            win.ShowAll ();

            Application.Run ();
    }

    static void Quit(object o, EventArgs args)
    {
            Application.Quit ();
    }
```

```
static void End_Delete(object o, DeleteEventArgs args)
{
        Application.Quit ();
}
}
```

Putting together a menu bar is an easy task. First of all, we create the menu bar itself. In the next step, some elements are added to the menu. We must distinguish between items and menus. Items can be bound to events and menus can contain items. Figure 15.8 shows what happens upon completion of the application.

FIGURE 15.8 The completion of the menus application.

Adjusting VScales

Scales are discussed extensively in many tutorials because they're a good way to demonstrate the interactions between various objects.

In this section, we take a brief look at scales so that you learn to use them efficiently. Let's start with an example:

```
using System;
using System.Drawing;
using Gtk;
using GtkSharp;

public class Demo
{
        static VScale vscale;

        public static void Main (string[] args)
        {
                Application.Init();
                Window win = new Window("Window");
                win.DefaultSize = new Size (250, 200);
                win.BorderWidth = 20;

                HBox box = new HBox(false, 2);

                Label label = new Label ("Scrollbar ...");
                box.PackStart (label, false, false, 0);

                Adjustment adj1 = new Adjustment (0.0, 0.0,
                                101.0, 0.1, 1.0, 1.0);
```

```
                        vscale = new VScale ((Adjustment) adj1);

                        vscale.DrawValue = true;
                        box.PackStart (vscale, true, true, 0);
                        vscale.ShowAll ();

                        Button button = new Button ("Reporting value");
                        button.Clicked += new EventHandler(GetValue);
                        box.Add(button);

                        win.Add (box);
                        win.ShowAll ();

                        Application.Run ();
            }

            static void GetValue(object o, EventArgs args)
            {
                        Console.WriteLine("Value: " + vscale.Value);
                        Application.Quit ();
            }
}
```

FIGURE 15.9   Scales.

We generate an instance of the Adjustment object. This object is used to define the scale. In the next step, we take the adjustment and assign it to the scale. Now we can make sure that the current value of the scale is displayed on screen. In addition to the scale, we display a button and assign an event to it. In the example shown in Figure 15.9, the current value of the button displays and the application quits. In this example, we use a VScale. However, it's also possible to use HScale instead.

In the next step, you can see how multiple elements can be combined with each other. Two scales should be combined with each other:

```
using System;
using System.Drawing;
using Gtk;
using GtkSharp;

public class Demo
{
```

```
public static void Main (string[] args)
{
        Application.Init();
        Window win = new Window("Window");
        win.DefaultSize = new Size (250, 200);
        win.BorderWidth = 20;

        HBox box = new HBox(false, 2);

        Label label = new Label ("Scrollbar ...");
        box.PackStart (label, false, false, 0);
        Adjustment justierung = new Adjustment (0.0, 0.0,
                        101.0, 0.1, 1.0, 1.0);
        VScrollbar scrollbar = new VScrollbar ((Adjustment) justierung);
        scrollbar.UpdatePolicy = UpdateType.Continuous;

        VScale vscale = new VScale ((Adjustment) justierung);
        vscale.DrawValue = true;
        box.PackStart (scrollbar, false, false, 0);
        box.PackStart (vscale, true, true, 0);
        vscale.ShowAll ();

        win.Add (box);
        win.ShowAll ();

        Application.Run ();
}
}
```

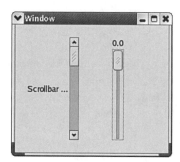

FIGURE 15.10   Scales again.

We create an instance of VScrollbar and an instance of VScale. Both instances are bound to the same adjustment. If one of the objects is changed, the second one is changed as well. Figure 15.10 shows what the result looks like.

Checkbuttons

Checkbuttons are an additional component that many people use to make their user interfaces more efficient. The GTK# libraries provide an object called CheckButton, which can be used to manage checkbuttons. Whenever a button is activated or deactivated, a method can be called to display a message:

```
using Gtk;
using GtkSharp;
using System;
using System.Drawing;

public class Demo
{
        public static void Main(string[] args)
        {
                Application.Init();

                Window window = new Window ("Buttons ...");
                window.BorderWidth = 10;
                window.DeleteEvent  += new DeleteEventHandler (delete_event);

                VBox box = new VBox(false, 0);
                box.BorderWidth = 10;

                // Creating buttons
                CheckButton checkbutton1 = new CheckButton ("CheckButton 1");
                CheckButton checkbutton2 = new CheckButton ("CheckButton 2");

                // Creating events
                checkbutton1.Clicked += new EventHandler (click_button);
                checkbutton2.Clicked += new EventHandler (click_button);

                box.PackStart(checkbutton1, false, false, 3);
                box.PackStart(checkbutton2, false, false, 3);

                window.Add(box);
                window.ShowAll();
                Application.Run();
        }

        static void delete_event(object obj, DeleteEventArgs args)
        {
                Application.Quit();
        }

        static void click_button(object obj, EventArgs args)
        {
                if (((CheckButton) obj).Active)
                {
```

```
                    Console.WriteLine ("activated");
        }
        else
        {
                    Console.WriteLine ("deactivated");
        }
    }
}
```

The constructor accepts the label of the check box as an input parameter. The events are defined as always. The result of the preceding code is shown in Figure 15.11. In our example, we define an event that informs us when somebody has clicked a button. To find out whether a checkbutton is active, we can look at Active.

FIGURE 15.11
Checkbuttons.

Selecting Files

Whenever it's necessary for the user to select a file, you must open a dialog from which the user can select the desired file on the hard disk. Therefore, GTK# provides objects that are ready for action. In the following code, we compile a brief example in which you can see how a file can be retrieved:

```
using Gtk;
using GtkSharp;
using System;
using System.Drawing;

public class Demo
{
        static FileSelection file_selection;

        static void sel_ok_event( object obj, EventArgs args )
        {
                Window erg_win = new Window("Result ...");
                erg_win.DefaultSize = new Size (250, 70);
                Label lab = new Label("Result: " + file_selection.Filename);
                erg_win.Add(lab);
                erg_win.ShowAll();
        }

        static void cancel_event (object obj, EventArgs args)
        {
                Window erg_win = new Window("Error");
```

```
        erg_win.DefaultSize = new Size (250, 70);
        Label lab = new Label("no file selected ...");
        erg_win.Add(lab);
        erg_win.ShowAll();
    }

    public static void Main(string[] args)
    {
        Application.Init ();
        file_selection = new FileSelection("Selection");
        file_selection.OkButton.Clicked
                +=new EventHandler(sel_ok_event);
        file_selection.CancelButton.Clicked
                += new EventHandler(cancel_event);

        file_selection.Filename = "logo.jpg";
        file_selection.Show();

        Application.Run();
    }
}
```

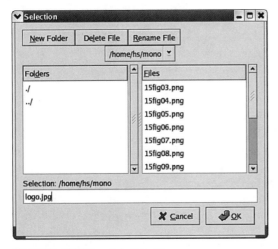

FIGURE 15.12   Selecting files.

The main program creates an instance of the FileSelection object, which displays a dialog for selecting a file on disk. All we have to do is to assign events to this instance so that Mono knows what to do with the file. Every button will be assigned to some action. Delegates are used to call various methods. Figure 15.12 contains an overview.

Additional Elements

GTK# provides a rich set of additional elements. Future versions of GTK# will provide all features that are provided by GTK. Because GTK# is built on GTK, the GTK# module can be developed fast and reliably.

Currently, GTK# is still under heavy development, so some errors might occur here and there. However, the development of GTK# is definitely going on, so users can benefit from good old technology.

Qt#

The Qt framework is widely used by the Open Source community. In contrast to GTK, the Qt libraries have not always been open. This led to many discussions in the community. Finally, the Qt libraries were released under the terms of the GPL license. A long and intense conflict between the developers of the KDE and the GNOME desktop has finally come to an end.

In this section, we focus on Qt# and you'll see how the Qt libraries can be easily used in combination with Mono.

Installation

Installing Qt# is an easy task and can be done quickly. In this section, you'll see how Qt# can be installed on Red Hat 8.0 systems.

The Installation Process

Before Qt# itself can be installed, we need some additional packages, such as the KDE bindings. You can find this package at `http://speakeasy.rpmfind.net/linux/RPM/redhat/8.0/i386/kdebindings-qtc-3.0.3-1.i386.html`. In the next step, Qt# can be downloaded from `http://qtcsharp.sourceforge.net`. Watch out: You need Qt# and QtC to make the system do its job.

The packages you just downloaded can be installed with the help of RPM:

```
rpm -Uvh *rpm
```

-U means installation or update. -v displays some information about the installation process. -h makes sure that hashes are displayed.

If no error occurs, the Qt# has been installed properly and you can almost start working.

If the process we just described does not work on your system, we recommend compiling the sources.

After the Installation

Just as for GTK#, you must set $MONO_PATH and LD_LIBRARY_PATH; otherwise, the system will not find the assemblies without additional hints.

Concepts

The Qt toolkit was originally developed by Troll Tech—a Norwegian company that focuses on graphics programming. The Qt framework makes writing platform-independent software comparatively simple so that you can use it safely on most platforms.

Qt provides what are known as *widgets*. This term is used for Unix as well as for Windows systems. Almost all elements describing the user interface are widgets, which can themselves contain widgets. Internally, all widgets are derived from a class called QWidget. Inside the program, it's easy to combine various elements.

Simple Windows

After this first brief overview, we'll take look at some basic examples. Here's some code:

```
using Qt;
using System;

public class MyButton : QVBox
{
        public static void Main (String[] args)
        {
                QApplication prog = new QApplication (args );
                MyButton hello = new MyButton ();
                prog.SetMainWidget (hello);
                hello.Show ();
                prog.Exec ();
        }

        public MyButton()
        {
                QPushButton pb = new QPushButton ("A text", this);
                QObject.Connect (pb, SIGNAL ("clicked()"), this,
                        SLOT("SlotClicked()"));
        }

        public void SlotClicked()
        {
                Console.WriteLine ("Button pressed");
        }
}
```

Inside the main function, we create an instance of the QApplication object. After that, we create a button called MyButton. The button itself is an instance of QPushButton. The text inside the button can be passed to the object as an instance. If you want to assign a method to the button, you can make use of Connect. If somebody clicks on a button, SlotClicked is started. In this example, text is displayed inside the button.

In the next step, `SetMainWidget` creates the main window. All elements are arranged and displayed by the system.

To compile the code, we need a simple command:

```
[hs@duron mono]$ mcs main.cs /r:Qt
Compilation succeeded
```

 This time we have to start the program with `mint` instead of Mono because otherwise some fatal errors would be displayed. Maybe this will be fixed in future versions of Mono. The simple window shown in Figure 15.13 will be displayed.

FIGURE 15.13
A simple window.

In the next example, we'll create two buttons:

```
using Qt;
using System;

public class MyButton : QVBox
{
        public static void Main (String[] args)
        {
                QApplication prog = new QApplication (args );

                QPushButton one = new QPushButton
                        ("text 1", null);
                QPushButton two = new QPushButton
                        ("text 2", null);

                one.Resize(150, 100);
                one.SetFont (new QFont ("Times", 15,
                        QFont.Weight.Bold));

                two.Resize(50, 50);

                prog.SetMainWidget (one);
                // prog.SetMainWidget (two);
                one.Show ();
                two.Show ();
                prog.Exec ();
        }
}
```

At the beginning of the application, an instance of QApplication is created. After that, we define buttons just as we've done before.

Now the first button is modified by changing the size of the text as well as the font. The second button is modified as well. With the help of SetMainWidget, we can define whether both windows should be closed when somebody closes one window. Finally, all elements are displayed as in Figure 15.14.

In the previous example, the buttons were displayed in two small windows. This is not what it's supposed to be, so we've included an example showing how both buttons can be displayed in one main window:

FIGURE 15.14   Two buttons.

```
using Qt;
using System;

public class MyButton : QVBox
{
        public static void Main (String[] args)
        {
                QApplication prog = new QApplication (args );

                QVBox box = new QVBox ();
                box.Resize (200, 120);

                QPushButton one = new QPushButton ("text 1", box);
                one.SetFont (new QFont("Times", 18, QFont.Weight.Bold));

                QPushButton two = new QPushButton ("text 2", box);

                box.Show ();
                prog.Exec ();
        }
}
```

This time we define a QVBox. Its height is 120 pixels, and its width is 200 pixels. The buttons are added to the box. This can be done with the help of the second parameter of the constructor of the QPushButton object.

To display the elements on screen, we use a method called Show. The layout of the window can be seen in Figure 15.15.

FIGURE 15.15   Two buttons in one window.

As you can see, our button will use the entire space in the window. In many cases, this isn't what you've been looking for. In the next example, you can see how buttons can be arranged differently:

```
using System;
using Qt;

public class Win : QWidget
{
        public Win (QWidget parent, String name) : base (parent, name)
        {
                this.SetMinimumSize(100, 100);
                this.SetMaximumSize(200, 150);

                // the first button ...
                QPushButton quit = new QPushButton("Quit",
                                this, "quit");
                quit.SetGeometry(10, 10, 80, 80);
                quit.SetFont(new QFont("Times", 12,
                                QFont.Weight.Normal));
                Connect(quit, SIGNAL("clicked()"), qApp,
                                SLOT("Quit()") );

                // the second button ...
                QPushButton end = new QPushButton("End", this, "end");
                end.SetGeometry(60, 60, 140, 140);
                end.SetFont(new QFont ("Times", 12,
                                QFont.Weight.Normal) );
                Connect(end, SIGNAL("clicked()"), qApp,
                                SLOT("Quit()") );
        }

        public Win(QWidget parent) : this (parent, "")
        {
        }

        public Win() : this (null, "")
        {
        }
}

public class Demo
{
```

```
public static void Main (String[] args)
{
        QApplication a = new QApplication(args);

        Win w = new Win();
        w.SetGeometry(100, 100, 200, 120);
        a.SetMainWidget(w);
        w.Show();
        a.Exec();
}
}
```

At the beginning of the program, we implement a class that displays the desired elements. In addition, we define the minimum and the maximum size that the window should have. We also define two buttons. Every button has a fixed size and a fixed position. The font we use for displaying the text is modified and a function is called whenever somebody clicks the button.

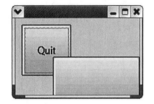

In the main program, we create an instance of Win. Then we define a size and assign the main window to the application. Finally all objects are displayed as shown in Figure 15.16.

As you can see in Figure 15.16, buttons can overlap. This is an important fact. In addition, it's possible to define buttons that are actually outside the window.

FIGURE 15.16 Freely arranged buttons.

Building Menus

As we have already seen in the section on GTK#, user interfaces are essential components of every desktop application. Defining menus is extraordinarily important. With the help of C# and Qt#, building menus is quite simple. In the next few examples, we focus on user interfaces that provide all kinds of menus.

Let's get started with a quick look at a simple application:

```
using Qt;
using System;

public class Menuleiste : QMainWindow
{
        private QMenuBar menubar;
        private QPopupMenu MenuOne, Desc;

        public Menuleiste ()
        {
```

```
            MenuOne = new QPopupMenu (null, "MenuOne");
            MenuOne.InsertItem      ("&Quit", qApp,
                    SLOT ("quit()"));

            Desc = new QPopupMenu(null, "Desc");
            Desc.InsertItem("&Notice", this,
                    SLOT("slotNotice()"));
            Desc.InsertItem("&Ein Error", this,
                    SLOT("slotError()"));

            menubar = new QMenuBar(this, "");
            menubar.InsertItem("&MenuItem", MenuOne);
            menubar.InsertItem("&Notice", Desc);
            menubar.InsertItem("&MenuItem", MenuOne);
    }

    public void slotNotice ()
    {
            QMessageBox.Information (this, "text",
                    "more text");
    }

    public void slotError ()
    {
            QMessageBox.Information (this, "Error",
                    "a fatal error Error");
    }

    public static void Main (String[] args)
    {
            QApplication anw = new QApplication (args);
            Menuleiste window = new Menuleiste ();
            window.SetCaption ("Header");
            anw.SetMainWidget (window);
            window.Show ();
            anw.Exec ();
            return;
    }
}
```

In the main function, we create an instance of an object called Menuleiste. This object contains the entire menu. Building the menu itself is an easy task. All we have to do is to call the InsertItem method to make sure that entries are added to the menu. Whenever a certain entry is supposed to perform some action, we have to use slots. Slots are an essential concept in Qt#. In general, slots are some sort of plug that you can use to tell Qt# that a certain method should be called.

FIGURE 15.17
A Qt#-driven menu.

In our case, we call `slotError` and `slotNotice`. When somebody selects an entry, a window containing a message will be displayed. In Qt#, a message box is an instance of `QMessageBox`. The first parameter of the `QMessageBox` constructor tells the window which object to use ("this" is used). The second and the third parameter tells Mono about the content of the window. If you want to define the caption of the main window, all you have to do is to call `SetCaption`.

Figure 15.17 shows what the main window will look like.

Text Fields

In this section, we describe how text fields can be displayed. Text fields are essential because they're necessary for processing long text. With the help of C#, it's almost trivial to implement a simple editor because most of the work has already been done.

In the following example, we examine a simple editor. To keep the code simple and easy to understand, we haven't implemented methods for loading and saving files. Let's have a look at the code:

```
using Qt;
using System;

public class Win : QMainWindow
{
        private TextArea textfield;

        private class TextArea : QTextEdit
        {
                public TextArea (QWidget parent) : base (parent)
                {
                        QFile file = new QFile ("/tmp/mytext");
                        if      ( file.Open(1) )
                        {
                                QTextStream text =
                                        new QTextStream (file);
                                this.SetText (text.Read ());
                                this.SetTabStopWidth (30);
                        }
                }
```

```
        }

        public Win ()
        {
                textfield = new TextArea (this);
                textfield.SetGeometry(0, 0, 100, 100);
                this.SetCentralWidget (textfield);
        }

        public static void Main (String[] args)
        {
                QApplication anw = new QApplication (args);
                Win myvi = new Win ();
                myvi.SetCaption ("Micro Vi 0.1");
                anw.SetMainWidget (myvi);
                myvi.Show ();
                anw.Exec ();
        }
}
```

The Win object makes sure that a text area is created. The target of the application is to open a file called /tmp/mytext. Therefore, we use an instance of QFile. Opening a file with Qt#'s onboard tools is pretty similar to using Mono's onboard tools. After opening the file, we create a stream. The text inside the file is added to the text area. All we have to do now is to define the size of the window and assign the text area to the main window. Figure 15.18 shows what the final result will look like.

FIGURE 15.18 Read the text carefully.

Additional Elements

Qt# provides a rich set of additional features. In this section, we focus on some of the most important features that we haven't discussed yet.

Grouping Elements

Before we get to some new elements you haven't seen yet, let's see how elements can be combined.

The next example shows how three elements can be combined. All elements will be displayed in one window. The example shows elements that you've already seen in this chapter.

```csharp
using Qt;
using System;

public class Win : QMainWindow
{
        private TextArea textfeld;

        private class TextArea : QTextEdit
        {
                public TextArea (QWidget parent) : base (parent)
                {
                        QFile file = new QFile ("/tmp/mytext");
                        if      ( file.Open(1) )
                        {
                                QTextStream text =
                                        new QTextStream (file);
                                this.SetText (text.Read ());
                                this.SetTabStopWidth (30);
                        }
                }
        }

        public Win ()
        {
                textfeld = new TextArea (this);
                textfeld.SetGeometry(0, 50, 200, 200);

                QSlider slider = new QSlider (Orientation.Horizontal,
                        this, "slider");
                slider.SetGeometry(0, 0, 50, 20);

                QLCDNumber lcd = new QLCDNumber (1, this, "lcd" );
                lcd.SetGeometry(50, 20, 80, 50);
        }

        public static void Main (String[] args)
        {
                QApplication anw = new QApplication (args);
                Win myvi = new Win ();
                myvi.SetCaption ("Micro Vi 0.1");
                anw.SetMainWidget (myvi);
                myvi.Show ();
```

```
                    anw.Exec ();
        }
}
```

The structure of the program should already be familiar to you. All we've done is to add two elements to the editor that you've seen before. Each element has a predefined size and a fixed position. That's the gist of this example because, in many cases, creating elements is much easier than arranging them. In this example, all elements are added to this object. this means that the current instance is taken. However, it's no problem to use another window if one is available in your application.

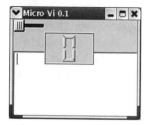

In our example, a scale is combined with a text field and an instance of the QLCDNumber object. If you want to assign certain tasks to the elements you've defined, feel free to use slots. You already saw how this works earlier in this section.

When you run the program, the strange window shown in Figure 15.19 will be displayed.

FIGURE 15.19
Interesting new applications.

Check Boxes

This section is dedicated to check boxes. The following example shows how check boxes can be displayed and how the current status of an element can be retrieved:

```
using Qt;
using System;

public class Win : QMainWindow
{
        public Win ()
        {
                QCheckBox check = new QCheckBox("Checkbox",
                        this, "check");
                check.SetGeometry(20, 20, 80, 80);
                check.SetChecked(true);

                Console.WriteLine("Status: " + check.IsChecked() );
        }

        public static void Main (String[] args)
        {
                QApplication anw = new QApplication (args);
                Win myvi = new Win ();
                myvi.SetCaption ("Elements ...");
```

```
            anw.SetMainWidget (myvi);
            myvi.Show ();
            anw.Exec ();
    }
}
```

Within the Qt# framework, check boxes can be created with the help of the QCheckBox object. The first parameter of the constructor helps you to define the text that's related to the check box. The parent object is defined by the second parameter. Again we use the current window as the parent. After that, we assign a name. To tell Mono how much space we want to use, we call SetGeometry.

Check boxes can be activated. To activate an element, we need to call SetChecked. All we have to do is to pass a Boolean value to the method. Now that we've told the check box that it's active, we try to find out about its status. This can be done with the help of IsChecked. In this example, the status of the check box is sent to standard output. If you want the result of IsChecked to be displayed in a small window, you can use the following piece of code:

```
Console.WriteLine("Status: " + check.IsChecked() );
QMessageBox.Information (this, "Notice ...",
        "Status: " + check.IsChecked());
```

FIGURE 15.20   A simple check box.

QMessageBox.Information makes sure that an additional widget is displayed before starting the main windows. Without this tiny extra feature, the main window would look like Figure 15.20.

When we start the application, the text is correctly displayed on the screen. Again, we use mint to call the application because using mono would lead to errors.

QCheckBox provides a set of additional methods, which are essential for your daily life with Qt#. Because those methods are so important, we decided to compile an overview:

- QCheckBox.DrawButton

- QCheckBox.DrawButtonLabel

- QCheckBox.Finalize

- QCheckBox.IsChecked

- QCheckBox.IsTristate

- QCheckBox.SetChecked

- QCheckBox.SetNoChange

- `QCheckBox.SetTristate(bool)`

- `QCheckBox.SetTristate()`

- `QCheckBox.UpdateMask`

In Brief

- Mono can be used in combination with various libraries for designing user interfaces such as Qt# and GTK#.

- Because of technical reasons, Windows-compliant forms are not supported yet.

- GTK# is based on the GTK libraries, which are widely used by GNOME developers.

- Qt# is based on the Qt libraries, which are widely used by KDE developers.

- Because of a bug in Mono, you have to use `mint` to run programs containing graphical user interfaces.

- GTK# and Qt# are separate modules and must be downloaded from the Internet.

- Both modules can be used with Windows and Unix operating systems.

Unsafe Code

Until now, we've seen what is called *safe code*. Safe code means that we have used a high abstraction level. Some C programmers among you will have noticed that we haven't used pointers up to now. Pointers are a real source of trouble. In C code, problems related to pointers are hard to find and lead to unpredictable errors. Therefore, C# tries to get rid of pointers whenever it's possible to do so. The problem with pointers is that internal pointers can damage almost everything that's within the scope of an application.

In this chapter, we deal with what is known as *unsafe code*.

Fundamentals

As we already mentioned, Mono supports two different types of code: safe code and unsafe code. The idea behind safe code is that there is no unsafe code in it, which means that it's some sort of pointer-free area. There are some additional restrictions, but pointers are definitely the most important one.

When talking about safe and unsafe code, people often think about managed and unmanaged code. To make those terms a little bit clearer, we have included a simple overview:

- Safe code: Safe code means that it can be executed safely without killing an entire application because of troubles related to memory management and pointers.

- Unsafe code: Within unsafe code, it's possible to use pointers and other unsafe features. Unsafe code has to be marked as such.

- Managed code: Code is usually managed code, which means that it's executed under the control of the common language runtime. All data types are managed on the heap.

- Unmanaged code: Unmanaged code is native code that is not executed under the control of the common language runtime.

It's important to understand the major differences between those types of code because it massively influences your daily work.

Pointers

In this section, we focus on pointers and you learn to use them safely. Many of you who have programmed in C extensively won't find too much new information.

Internally, a pointer is nothing else than a guide to an object. In other words, a pointer contains the address of an object in memory. Pointers are low-level stuff, so you'll have to deal with addresses. That's the reason why pointers are dangerous: Data can easily be put into the wrong part of the memory.

Fundamental Operations and Basics

Now it's time to look at an example so that you can see how to work with pointers and addresses:

```
using System;

public class Demo
{
        unsafe static void Main()
        {
                int i = 10;
                int *j;

                j = &i;
                i = 20;

                Console.WriteLine("i: {0} - j: {1}", i, *j);
        }
}
```

The main function has been marked as unsafe because we use pointers inside it. At the beginning of the application, we define an integer variable. After that, we create a pointer. The

pointer contains nothing more than the address of the object in memory. When we use an *
in front of the variable, we follow the pointer and retrieve the value of the variable that the
pointer points to. When the * is removed, the address of the object can be accessed.

When working with pointers, the & (ampersand) operator is important. It can be used to
retrieve the address of a variable.

Let's have a quick overview: The * operator can be used to retrieve the value at a certain
address. The & operator is necessary to find the address of a value. In our example, we assign
the address of i to j. In other words, we clone the variable. When the value of i is changed,
the value of j also changes. We want to point out that, at the end of the program, j is not
just a copy of i but is the same variable—the same piece of memory is accessed.

To compile the program, an additional compiler flag is needed: We have to tell the compiler
that we use unsafe code, so /unsafe has to be added to the command line:

```
[hs@duron mono]$ mcs /unsafe main.cs
Compilation succeeded
```

When starting the program, the result looks like this:

```
[hs@duron mono]$ mono main.exe
i: 20 - j: 20
```

The result meets our expectations because the second variable is nothing more than an alias.

Pointers, Mathematics, and Dangers

A pointer points to a certain element in memory. In some situations, you might want to find
out which object you can find next to this object. With the help of some simple math, a
pointer can be moved. Imagine a simple string. A string is a *reference type*, which means that
it can be identified by its starting address. So, the main idea is to take the pointer, increment
the memory address it points to, and see what happens. That's the purpose of the next
program:

```
using System;

public class Demo
{
        unsafe static void Main()
        {
                string str = "Hello";
                fixed (char *p = str);

                for     (int i = 0; i < str.Length + 5; i++)
                {
```

```
                    Console.WriteLine("p: {0}", *p);
                    p++;
            }
        }
}
```

At the beginning of the program, we define a string. After that, we define a pointer that points to the string. In this case, we use a keyword. `fixed` makes sure that the pointer cannot be lost when the string is moved inside the memory. When running `Concat`, this can happen easily. Then we go through every element of the string and display it on the screen. To show you what might happen when more data is retrieved from memory, we display five additional characters. In this example, these fields are empty.

Again, we have to use /`unsafe` to compile the code:

```
[hs@duron mono]$ mono main.exe
p: H
p: e
p: l
p: l
p: o
p:
p:
p:
p:
p:
```

Reading memory is not dangerous. However, writing data into memory can lead to unexpected side effects that might lead to core dumps or severe errors. The kernel makes sure that no memory belonging to other applications can be destroyed, but inside the memory belonging to the application itself, the situation is different.

Addresses and Friends

When debugging an application, it can be necessary to display the address of an object. As you can see in the next listing, this can be done easily:

```
using System;

public class Demo
{
        unsafe static void Main()
        {
```

```
        int x = 100;
        int *ptr = &x;

        Console.WriteLine("Address: {0}", (int) ptr);
        Console.WriteLine("Value: {0}", *ptr);
    }
}
```

To display an address in hex format, we could have used this:

```
Console.WriteLine("Adresse: {0:X}", (int) ptr);
```

Let's get back to the original application. At the beginning of the program, we create an integer value. In the next step, we define a pointer and assign the address of the integer value to it. This can be done with the help of the & operator.

The output of the program looks like this:

```
[hs@duron mono]$ mono main.exe
Address: 1096861864
Value: 100
```

Pointers and Functions

Pointers are often used to pass data to functions. In the section about references, we already saw how this can be done. However, we have not used pointers yet. In this section, we see how data can be passed to a function with the help of pointers. Mono works pretty similarly to C, so it isn't too difficult to understand:

```
using System;

public class Demo
{
        unsafe static void Main()
        {
                int x = 3;
                int y = 7;

                Console.WriteLine("x: {0} - y: {1}", x, y);
                swap(&x, &y);
                Console.WriteLine("x: {0} - y: {1}", x, y);
        }

        unsafe static void swap(int *a, int *b)
        {
```

```
        int c = *a;
        *a = *b;
        *b = c;
    }
}
```

We pass the addresses of x and y to swap. This function simply swaps the content of those two values. We need just three statements to do the job. The most important thing is that the data is changed permanently—the changes won't be lost at the end of the function.

Here is the proof:

```
[hs@duron mono]$ mono main.exe
x: 3 - y: 7
x: 7 - y: 3
```

sizeof

An additional feature that can be used only in unsafe code deals with objects and sizes. Mono provides the keyword sizeof, which does nothing other than return the size of an object in bytes. As you can see in the next example, sizeof can be used easily:

```
using System;

public class Demo
{
        static void Main()
        {
                double x = 3241.15;
                unsafe
                {
                        byte *y = (byte*) &x;

                        for (int i = 0; i < sizeof(double); ++i)
                        {
                                Console.Write("{0} - {1,4}",
                                        i, (uint) (*y++));
                                Console.WriteLine();
                        }
                }
        }
}
```

Sometimes the entire function isn't based on unsafe code. In many cases, it can be useful to mark only a few pieces as unsafe. In our example, a double is defined in the safe code. In the unsafe block, we create a pointer and assign a value to it. After that, we process every byte one after the other. Inside the loop, we display some information about the current byte.

Let's look at the output of the program:

```
[hs@duron mono]$ mono main.exe
0 -  205
1 -  204
2 -  204
3 -  204
4 -   76
5 -   82
6 -  169
7 -   64
```

As you can see, it's easy to process a variable byte after byte.

stackalloc

When working with pointers, memory might have to be allocated explicitly. In C, this job is done by functions such as `malloc` and `alloca` (which is the counterpart of `stackalloc`). Mono and .NET provide an alternative method called `stackalloc` to do the job. However, when working with Mono it isn't necessary to free memory manually because everything is done by the garbage collection unless memory is allocated explicitly with the help of `stackalloc`.

In the next example, you can see how `stackalloc` can be called:

```
using System;

public class Demo
{
        unsafe static void Main()
        {
                string input = "Mono";
                char *a = stackalloc char[input.Length];
                char *p = a;

                foreach (char c in input)
                {
                        *p = c;
```

```
                    Console.WriteLine(*p);
                    p++;
            }
        }
    }
```

The code in the example you just saw does not compile on some versions of Mono. If your version of mcs does not compile the code properly, you should try it with a different version.

In this example, you can see how stackalloc can be used correctly. Inside the loop, we use the memory we just allocated. In the next listing, you can see what the output will look like when starting the program:

```
[hs@duron mono]$ mono main.exe
M
o
n
o
```

After that short example, let's look at an additional example that does exactly the same thing:

```
using System;

public class Demo
{
    unsafe static void Main()
    {
        string input = "Mono";
        char *a = stackalloc char[1];
        char *p = a;

        for (int i = 0; i < 300000; i++)
        {
            *p = input[0];
            Console.WriteLine(*p);
            p++;
        }
    }
}
```

That's not the way pointers should be used. In this example, we do everything we can to access memory we aren't allowed to access because it has not been allocated with the help of stackalloc. In C, this would lead to a wonderful core dump.

In case of Mono, the situation is different:

```
Unhandled Exception: System.NullReferenceException: A null value was
found where an object instance was required
in <0x0005d> 00 .Demo:Main ()
```

Mono reports an error and terminates the application instantly.

PInvoke

Mono enables us to use native code inside an application. Up to now, we've seen how Mono can be used to write ordinary applications. In this section, you learn to combine Mono with other software packages.

Basic Concepts

We've already mentioned that the C# compiler does not produce native code, but instead produces intermediate code. The advantage of this concept is that all languages that have an interface to .NET can be used in combination with Mono. But what can people do with code that isn't based on .NET? Software components have often been used for a long time and been extensively tested. It's definitely not a good idea to throw away code that still does a good job.

The solution is that Mono provides interfaces to external code. All you have to do is to include an external module into Mono to use it. This reduces the costs of software development significantly and helps you to raise the stability of your applications because you can use well-tested and stable code.

In this section, we take a closer look at Mono's interface to the C programming language. This opens a broad range of possibilities and your application can get an additional performance boost.

Extending Mono with C

The most widespread languages for extending Mono seems to be C and C++, respectively. The Mono framework provides an easy to use interface, so integrating C code is no problem at all.

Simple Extensions

The target of the next example is to implement a shared object that computes the sum of two numbers. The C function for this calculation is very simple:

```
#include <stdio.h>
```

```
int sum(int a, int b)
{
        return a + b;
}
```

We pass two parameters to the function. The sum of those two parameters is returned. To compile the code, you can use good old gcc and a makefile:

```
libsum.so       :       sum.c Makefile
        gcc -Wall -fPIC -O2 -c -o libsum.o sum.c
        gcc -shared -Wl,-soname,libsum.so -o libsum.so libsum.o
```

The result of this operation is a file named libsum.so. We can use this file and integrate it into Mono:

```
using System;
using System.Runtime.InteropServices;

public class Demo
{
        [DllImport ("libsum.so", EntryPoint="sum")]
        static extern int sum(int a, int b);

        unsafe static void Main()
        {
                int x = sum(23, 45);
                Console.WriteLine("x: {0}", x);
        }
}
```

In this example, using EntryPoint=sum isn't absolutely necessary, but doing so adds some extra documentation to the file.

DllImport tells Mono that we want to import a shared object. In addition, an entry point is defined. DllImport supports some additional flags, which are compiled in the following list:

- CallingConvention: Defines the calling convention that has to be used. The default value of this setting is Winapi.

- CharSet: Defines the character set that should be used.

- EntryPoint: Defines the entry point.

- ExactSpelling: Tells Mono whether the entry point must be correctly spelled. The default value is False.

- **PreserveSig**: Tells us whether the signature of a method should be changed.

- **SetLastError**: Defines whether the last error should be preserved. The default value is zero.

After importing the shared object, we have to declare the functions we're planning to use. Therefore, we use what are called *prototypes*. Inside the main function, we can easily access the module.

The next example shows that this feature works really well:

```
[hs@duron test]$ mono unsafe.exe
x: 68
```

In the previous example, we chose a very simple C program that works with integer variables. In case of more complicated applications, this just isn't enough. In the next example, we take a look at a more complex data type. In C, strings are represented as character arrays.

Let's start with a simple example:

```
#include <stdio.h>
#include <string.h>

int debug (char *s)
{
        printf("Output: %s\n", s);
        return 0;
}
```

This function displays a string on the screen. As you can see, the string is defined by a pointer pointing to the first element in the string. Therefore, the way parameters are passed to the function is essential. As you can see, we use a pointer. Inside the function, we can write ordinary C code.

To test the function, you can use a simple piece of C# code:

```
using System;
using System.Text;
using System.Runtime.InteropServices;

public class Demo
{
        [DllImport ("libsum.so",
                EntryPoint="debug")]
        static extern int debug(string sb);
```

```
        unsafe static void Main()
        {
                int x = debug("hello");
        }
}
```

The shared object is again imported with the help of DllImport. This time a string is passed to the C function. Inside the C# program, we can call the function directly.

To compile the program, we can use the makefile you saw before. In addition, the C# file has to be compiled, which should be an easy task:

```
[hs@duron unsafe]$ mcs --unsafe unsafe.cs
Compilation succeeded
[hs@duron unsafe]$ mono unsafe.exe
Output: hello
```

Runtime Considerations

Why should somebody extend Mono with the help of a C program? Well, the most important reason is that there is already a huge amount of well-tested C code around, so you can rely on good old technology and build your applications on top of it. This enables you to migrate to Mono fast.

An additional point is that C code is fast. Modern C compilers are highly developed and highly optimized tools. In most situations, C is much more efficient than any other language around, so using C might help you to significantly improve the performance of your C# application.

Passing Structures and Objects to External Functions

It's absolutely no problem to pass objects or structures to external functions. This is essential because in C# almost everything is an object; otherwise, using external C code would not be possible. However, we don't deal with external objects in this book because they are far beyond the scope of an introduction.

In Brief

- Mono can be extended with C/C++

- *Safe code* means that it can be executed safely without killing an entire application because of troubles related to memory management and pointers.

- Within unsafe code, it's possible to use pointers and other unsafe features. Unsafe code has to be marked as such.

- Code is usually *managed* code, which means that it's executed under the control of the common language runtime. All data types are managed on the heap.

- Unmanaged code is native code that is not executed under the control of the common language runtime.

- To import a C library, you have to call `DllImport`.

- To import a function, you can call `PInvoke`.

Index

Symbols

& (ampersand) operator, 271
* (asterisk) operator, 271
[=] (equals) operator, 24

A

abstract classes, 90-92
accessing
    data via ADO.NET, 209
    DateTime object attributes, 200-201
    multiple variable values, 76-77
adding
    characters to strings, 141
    data to PostgreSQL tables, 213-214
Adjustment object, 250
ADO.NET
    accessing data, 209
    architecture, 207
    classes, 209
    offline access, 209
ampersand (&) operator, 271
analyzing objects, 77-80
    MemberInfo object, 83
    MethodInfo object, 81-82

compilers

C#, 2, 6

compiler flags, 51-52

compiling files, 49

compiling multiple files, 49-50

escaping characters, 20-22

JIT, 2

debugging applications, 61

MSIL, 4-5

compiling

files, 49-51

regular expressions, precompiling, 154

strings, 145-146

unsafe code, 271

Concat method, 136

connecting

strings, 135-136

to CVS servers, 9

connection-oriented protocols (network programming), 172

constants, 36

constructor functions, 34

constructors

DateTime object constructors, 197-198

TimeSpan object constructors, 201

ContextMarshalException class, 57

converting strings, 142-144

copying strings, 137-138

CryptoStream class, 121

cursors, 222-223

CVS servers, connecting to, 9

D

data, PostgreSQL tables

inserting into, 213-214

updating in, 214-215

data providers, 208

data structures. *See also* **value types**

implementing, 101-103

interfaces, 111

System.Collections namespace, 103-111

versus classes, 103

data types, 5

predefined data types, 15-17

reference types, 47-48

value types, 46

databases

accessing data, ADO.NET, 209

cursors, 222-223

exception handling, 219

inserting data, 213-214

metadata, 219-222

PostgreSQL database connections, 210-211

simple queries, 215-218

stored procedures, 223-225

tables, creating, 212

transactions, 222

updating data, 214-215

dates, comparing, 198-199

DateTime class

dates, comparing, 198-199

DateTime object, static methods, 200-201

leap years, 199-200

hiding, 40-41

importing, Pinvoke, 280

Main function, debugging applications, 61-62

overloading, 224-225

pointers, 273

G

GetBytes method, 143

goto command, 26

graphics, displaying near window borders, 241-243

displaying via GTK# interface, 241

grouping elements, Qt# interface, 263-265

GTK# interface, 237

checkbuttons, 251-253

elements, 254

events, 240-241

images, displaying, 241

installing, 238

menus, 247-249

scales, 249-251

scrollable windows, 240

selecting files, 253-254

simple windows

assigning events to buttons, 239

defining event handlers, 240

drawing, 238-239

tables, 246-247

windows

adding multiple elements, 242-243

assigning events to buttons, 239

defining borders, 243

defining event handlers, 240

drawing, 238-239

frames, 244-246

labels, 244-246

H - I

handling exceptions

AppDomainUnloadedException class, 57

ApplicationException class, 57

ArgumentException class, 57

ArgumentNullException class, 57

ArgumentOutOfRangeException class, 57

ArithmeticException class, 57

ArrayTypeMismatchException class, 57

BadImageFormatException class, 57

CannotUnloadAppDomainException class, 57

catch keyword, 53, 55

checked keyword, 59-60

ContextMarshalException class, 57

DivideByZeroException class, 57

DllNotFoundException class, 57

DuplicateWaitObjectException class, 57

EntryPointNotFoundException class, 57

Exception class, 57

ExecutionEngineException class, 57

FieldAccessException class, 57

finally keyword, 56

FormatException class, 57

IndexOutOfRangeException class, 57

How can we make this index more useful? Email us at indexes@samspublishing.com

Your Guide to Computer Technology

www.informit.com

KICK START

< QUICK >

< CONCISE >

< PRACTICAL >

Microsoft Visual Basic .NET 2003 Kick Start

By Duncan Mackenzie

0-672-32549-7

$34.99 US/$54.99 CAN

Microsoft Visual C#.NET 2003 Kick Start

By Steve Holzner

0-672-32547-0

$34.99 US/$54.99 CAN

ASP.NET Data Web Controls Kick Start

By Scott Mitchell

0-672-32501-2

$34.99 US/$54.99 CAN

Tomcat Kick Start

By Martin Bond and Debbie Law

0-672-32439-3

$34.99 US/$54.99 CAN

Struts Kick Start

By James Turner and Kevin Bedell

0-672-32472-5

$34.99 US/$54.99 CAN

EJB 2.1 Kick Start

By Peter Thaggard

0-672-32178-5

$34.99 US/$54.99 CAN

JAX: Java APIs for XML Kick Start

By Aoyon Chowdhury and Parag Choudhary

0-672-32434-2

$34.99 US/$54.99 CAN

JSTL: JSP Standard Tag Library Kick Start

By Jeff Heaton

0-672-32450-4

$34.99 US/$54.99 CAN